Beyond Room 109

Developing Independent Study Projects

Richard Kent

Boynton/Cook Publishers
HEINEMANN
Portsmouth, NH

For Pam and Fred,
whose love and support
have enriched my life.

Boynton/Cook Publishers, Inc.
A subsidiary of Reed Elsevier Inc.
361 Hanover Street
Portsmouth, NH 03801–3912
www.boyntoncook.com

Offices and agents throughout the world

© 2000 by Richard Kent

Library of Congress Cataloging-in-Publication Data
Kent, Richard Burt.
  Beyond room 109 : developing independent study projects / Richard Kent.
     p. cm.
  Includes bibliographical references and index.
  ISBN 0-86709-492-3
  1. Independent study—United States. 2. Project method in teaching.
  I. Title. II. Title: Beyond room one hundred nine.
  LB1049.K45   2000
  371.39'43—dc21
                                          99-42848
                                            CIP

Consulting Editor: Tom Newkirk
Production service: Colophon
Production coordination: Abigail M. Heim
Cover design: Michael Leary Design
Manufacturing: Deanna Richardson

Printed in the United States of America on acid-free paper
03   02   01   00   99   DA   1   2   3   4   5

Contents

Possibilities: An Introduction   v

Acknowledgments   vii

Section I   Preparing for Independent Study Projects

1   Preparing for ISP: In-Class Projects   1

2   Escaping: Out-of-School Projects   26

Section II   Independent Study Projects

3   ISP: The First Week   51

4   The Academic/Research ISP   66

5   Career ISP   69

6   Hobby/Life Passion ISP   83

7   Multitheme ISP   89

8   Selected Reading ISP   94

9   Questions and Concerns   100

10   Beyond Tomorrow   116

Appendix: At-a-Glance ISP Outlines   123

Works Cited   148

Index   150

Independent study, community service, adventures and experience, large doses of privacy and solitude, a thousand different apprenticeships, the one-day variety or longer—these are all powerful, cheap, and effective ways to start real reform of schooling.

John Taylor Gatto
Dumbing Us Down

We must get away from the "donation" metaphor of education in which teachers give and students receive. People learn by being involved, by doing things for themselves.

Theodore R. Sizer
Horace's Compromise

A Day in the Life Beyond 109

Today, most of my students are not in class. Sandra reads stories to a woman in an Alzheimer's unit. Ryan and Chad job-shadow a doctor, a graduate who is in residency at Maine Medical Center. Down the hallway from my classroom, Josie choreographs a lyrical dance while a few miles from school Roger, Dan, and Jason have discovered that building a log cabin is a whole lot tougher than they thought. At St. John's Elementary School, Sam An listens to a lively third grader as she reads a short passage. Back in Room 109, Darcy and Dusty make plans for a weekend journey to the home of the late author Louise Dickinson Rich. Her cabin sits on the shores of Rapid River in the thick pine woods of western Maine. Other of my students write letters to businesspeople, E-mail former students, and scroll through endless screen pages on the Internet. A few kids are lost or floundering. They wait for inspiration, their teacher, or mercifully, the end of the school year.

It's a typical day.

Possibilities: An Introduction

Good classrooms have all kinds of possibilities.

James Britton
The Bread Loaf School
of English

"How can you do a study of rock walls without building a rock wall?" I asked. Wendy and Kurt stared. I could sense they hoped that I would reconsider, or at the very least offer up a reprieve that did not include hours of hauling rocks on the last weekend of the school year. After all, throughout their independent study project they had read, biked, explored, composed, painted, journaled, photographed, and interviewed. Did they really need to fulfill this one last aspect of their project?

That Sunday, with graduation looming and the year-end blahs melting their ambition, Wendy and Kurt lugged, stacked, and arranged rocks on a searing summerlike day. Later that evening, while I was seated at my computer, the telltale *ping* and tiny red flag signaled E-mail. It was from Kurt. "Your rock wall is done."

Seven years ago I added independent study projects (ISP) to my English curriculum. I did so because of all the talk about school-to-work programs. I also initiated ISP because part of my job as a teacher is to help my students see themselves, and their future selves, more clearly. That's not always easy while seated in a classroom. And finally, quite frankly, ISP came about because my students and I needed a change from the day-to-day of classroom life.

In Wendy and Kurt's case, my role was simply to point out what I considered the obvious: Studying rock walls is different from building a rock wall. It seemed to me that it's good to experience both sides. Independent study projects allow just that.

So, during the last quarter of the school year, from late March through mid-June, my English students embark on journeys of discovery. A number of ISP are traditional research projects. Some are apprenticeships, and others could be considered internships. If this were Outward Bound, a few of my students' experiences might be akin to *solos*. Whatever they are called, these adventures allow my students to experience the world beyond the classroom walls in a meaningful way. Surely, after eleven or twelve years of schoolhouse schooling, it's high time.

In this book I show the range of independent study projects from my own high school teaching practice here in the western mountains of Maine. Before addressing these year-end projects, however, I share a number of activities from the first three quarters of the year. These programs, both in and out of school, usher my students toward the autonomy that independent study projects require. These experiences also help the teacher grow accustomed to working with and managing students outside the classroom.

While reading this book you may wonder about my school and town. The paper mill communities of Rumford and Mexico have a combined population of about ten thousand people. As one of my students wrote in his college admission's essay, "We don't have a mall, a movie theater, or even a Wal-Mart," but close by we have lakes, hiking trails, and ski areas. One thing I know firsthand, the river valley is a good place to raise children. This is where my sister, brothers, and I grew up.

Mountain Valley High School enrolls around 550 students, grades nine through twelve. In my mind, this makes the school just the right size for innovation. However, over the past ten years we have had seven principals and four assistant principals. This turnover has created a number of difficulties, not the least of which has been a scattered focus. Even so, when people visit our school the first thing they notice is how happy our students seem to be. That's because we have a hardworking staff that cares about kids.

Each day of the school year here at Mountain Valley High School, I work with future lawyers, loggers, and funeral directors in six heterogeneously grouped English classes of up to 120 students. I advise and guide, lure and supervise, cajole and teach, grumble and instruct while helping these young adults create a foundation for and connection to their future lives. This final nine weeks called ISP is not a curriculum-driven, institution-first model. This is about people and the lives they would lead.

Acknowledgments

Over the past few years, a number of my student colleagues have helped with the research and nitty-gritty of this book. Thanks to David Gallagher, Lincoln MacIsaac, Melissa Thibodeau, Aaron Fergola, Matthew Glazier, Matthew Kellogg, Chris Capponi, Kate Austin, Brandin Turner, Matthew Duguay, and Alissa Waite. Thanks also to the many Room 109 students who allowed me to tell their stories.

Each day, many of my colleagues throughout M.S.A.D. #43 strive to make school a place where children and their learning come first. I have learned much from these gifted practitioners, and for this I am forever grateful.

My friends in the Maine Writing Project listened to portions of this manuscript during our summer together. They offered thoughtful observations and encouragement. My thanks to them and to our indefatigable director, Jeff Wilhelm.

I will always owe a debt of gratitude to the Bread Loaf School of English. This uncommon place of learning helped me chart a course for an awesome journey of discovery. That journey happily continues with my new friends and colleagues at The Claremont Graduate University.

Tom Newkirk, my friend and Boynton/Cook editor, continues to guide with grace. Whether we are hiking Tumbledown Mountain, trading E-mail, or chatting in our respective classrooms, Tom moves me to new levels.

Once again, Anne Wood's editorial support and friendship have been invaluable. With this book I celebrate Anne's thirty-eighth year in teaching.

And to my family . . . you're simply the best.

1

Preparing for ISP: In-Class Projects

If you attend Mountain Valley High School, there's a good chance you know about independent study projects. You heard that Leah teaches kindergarten with Mrs. Doiron at Virginia Elementary School; that John, whose ISP is on flying, flew over my house on an early Sunday morning while I was washing my truck; and that Maia and Aaron traveled to Portland to interview a college professor who works with Maine's gay and lesbian population. You heard that while skiing Mount Washington's Tuckerman's Ravine, part of a study on the grand old New Hampshire mountain, Aaron crashed head-over-heels down its headwall, only to recover and laugh wildly with his ISP partner, E.J. You also heard *and* read in the local newspaper that Joel was caught and summonsed for taking more than the state limit of fish. (A first and hopefully a last for 109 ISP.)

Yes, if you attend Mountain Valley you know about ISP. To the outsider, these projects look like pure fun. Yet, independent study projects take a good deal of brooding and planning, not to mention a few restarts. The following activities and practices help prepare my students and me for their year-end "escapes."

Coming to Know My Students: Summer Letters and Autobiographies

Kristin knows she will enter the medical field, and Adam wants to be an athletic trainer. Judy will "never ever" live in a small mill town like Rumford, and Ryan is interested in the military police. And Sarah? Like so many of my students, Sarah hasn't a clue what she would like to do or be. Worse yet, some of my students just don't seem to care.

Learning about my students' interests and post–high school plans makes me a better ISP consultant—and a better English teacher. I like to touch base with my students before school starts. I write a letter every ten days and mail it to them from the high school. (Yes, it's the same letter for all one hundred-plus students! Yes, the school pays postage. No, this isn't necessary for a successful ISP; I just enjoy writing.) In a good year about 70 percent of my future students write back on a regular basis. Of course, they receive credit for this summer work.

In late August on the first day of class, I assign a five-page autobiography. The essay is a first-draft, spell-checked piece of expressive writing in which I encourage my students to discuss their plans for the future. As with the summer letters, I learn a lot.

I want to go to a four year college . . . then go on to medical school to study natural medicine (homeopathic) . . .

I had thoughts and dreams about playing in the NBA . . . before I knew what life was all about.

In the future I will find myself at Southern Maine Technical College.

I would like to be a Psychiatrist.

I am also a member of the Mountain Valley Amateur Radio Club.

I am pretty positive that my future occupation will have something to do with computers because they are like magnets and I am a paper clip.

I just want to be successful, be a decent person, and be someone to look up to.

I love to work with people less fortunate than me.

I am also interested in being a 911 dispatcher.

This past year I've been thinking about being a teacher.

After school I'm gonna keep on motocross racing. I will most likely make Pro by the end of this season.

I hope to touch many people's lives.

I want to experiment with hormones and other bodily chemicals to find if certain reactions in the brain cause a specific thought or feeling.

These glimpses into my students and their tomorrows help me individualize my teaching instruction and focus in on ISP ideas. I respond to each autobiography over the extended Labor Day weekend with a four- or five-paragraph letter. My purpose? I want my students to think about life's "every-anything" as possibility. I also want to show them that I care.

Making Connections:
It's Not Always *What* You Know . . .

I'm watching my high school soccer team warm up at an away match. A smiling man with a crew cut calls my name.

"I know I know you," I say. "Help me out."

"Jay Milton," he says. "I played for you in England on the state team."

The moment he tells me he is a videographer at a Portland television station my hand instinctively reaches around his shoulder. I feel like I'm selling swampland, but I won't let the moment slip by. "Listen, Jay. I have a student named Aaron who's deeply interested in film. Any chance he could spend a day with you?"

We swap phone numbers. The next day in school I track down Aaron; his eyes light up when I explain the possibilities. I have him call Jay from the school's office. It's an awkward phone call for this sixteen-year-old, but he survives and begins planning. Soon, I hope, he will truck off to the city of Portland to get an up-close look at the career he's been dreaming about.

The work involved for me? Sixty seconds of conversation at an away soccer match; ten minutes and a quick phone call back in school; three minutes to jot a note of thanks to Jay. In less than fifteen minutes, a young person has inched his foot a bit farther through the proverbial door.

An experience like Aaron's allows students to see themselves beyond high school looking at schools, careers, or life hobbies. Of course, Aaron might *not* become a videographer, but that's not the point. The experience is.

Utilizing everyday connections—family, friends, businesses, and community resources—helps create a rich pool of contacts for ISP students. I keep a list of those contacts and add to it every chance I get.

Life Work: Helping My Students Envision Their Futures

Joe is an entrepreneurial diamond miner who travels the world. JoAnne, a poet, tended the town dump where she set up an exchange program of books, furniture, and baby clothing. Eventually, she became a selectperson for her town of five hundred. John has worked thirty-four different jobs since his high school years while George, a thirty-year veteran of the Air Force, has lived all around our planet. Diane is an advocate for abused women; Jim played professional baseball.

One way we begin our year in Room 109 is by listening to people's Life Work stories. The talks are rich and wonderful, especially when viewed as a tapestry of lives. Listening to people's stories helps my students look forward to their own adult lives. Listening stimulates their dreaming and scheming while offering suggestions for careers and for ISP topics.

Setting up this classroom experience is not difficult. I ask my students during the first week of class to invite in anyone—everyone—to share their stories. Most think immediately of parents or relatives. One girl hopes to coax in her grandmother, a bartender for thirty years. We can only imagine her tales.

If Life Work sounds like an elementary school practice, you're right. Aren't elementary schools just the best places in the learning world? Anyway, since my high school has a block schedule, we have a certain flexibility with ninety-minute classes every other day. My classmates and I lure speakers from all walks of life. We ask for just ten minutes of their time to talk about what they've done for work and why. Sometimes when student interest is high or the speaker is quite comfortable, these conversations go on for up to forty-five minutes. That's rarely a scheduling problem. I set aside three weeks of the nine-week quarter for this segment of the Life Work theme. Sometimes we don't use all three weeks; other times a speaker or two straggles in during the fourth or fifth week. Again, we're flexible.

And no, all of the students do not invite people into class. This year we ended up averaging a total of nine speakers in each class over the three weeks. Overall, 25 percent of my students brought in Life Work guests. Because of the low numbers this year—all my fault because I didn't do a good job of encouraging my students as I have in the past—I arranged for school staff members and friends of mine from town to speak.

Among those guests, our school's principal shared his memories and wisdom of thirty-seven years in teaching. "One thing I've come to realize over the years," says Mr. Rowe, a former English teacher and baseball umpire, "it's not so much what you choose for a job or how much money you make; it's how you treat people that matters." One of our guidance counselors, Nancy Hall, spoke about her years of work in a hospital's accounts receivable department. "I didn't feel as if I was making a difference. That's when I began taking classes in education."

From these talks, discussions unfold. Two recurrent themes are service to others and money. And weaved through every conversation is the underlying theme of "a life well lived." During these discussions my students' views can be astounding and at times frightening.

"I want to touch people's lives," whispers Kristin, who in three weeks has only spoken once—while presenting a book project, a watercolor painting of an angel.

"For me, it's money, plain and simple," says an all-state athlete. "I want as much of it as possible, and I don't care how I get it."

"I can't see myself after high school," says Missy. "Whenever I think about it, I get confused. My gram thinks I should just find a guy with a good job and latch onto him."

This, I thought to myself, is one reason why we're doing what we're doing.

Some of the Life Work talks are ordinary, but as part of a collection they sing. Every once in a while we hit pay dirt, as with Jody's guest. Her dad suggested she invite the president of a consulting firm who happened to be working at the local paper mill. As with all top-notch professionals, Jack

Jacchino of the J. P. Burns Group is organized. Beyond his interesting perspectives on learning, work, and life, the notes he used to guide his talk helped me emphasize a point about success.

"Look at this," I said, holding up the one-page outline Jack prepared for his talk (see Figure 1–1). "Here you have the president of a company coming to speak with twenty-five teenagers. Look how organized he is."

I wasn't sure whether the kids understood, so I continued. "He could have just improvised—you know, spoken off the top of his head. But he prepared for you. He took you seriously. Successful people plan and take every opportunity with a certain seriousness." I ran to the main office and copied Jack's notes for my students.

One young woman who speaks during Life Work has just graduated from Bates College in Lewiston, Maine. Now she's enrolled in a teacher certification program and has been volunteering in my classroom. Colleen tells us of the variety of her jobs over the past seven years, from working at the Gap to lifeguarding on Nantucket. Two days after her talk, she brings in a short essay, saying, "I didn't give the whole story. This might help some of them." The essay tells us how Colleen failed a class during the final semester of her college career. The failure prevented her from graduating. The following is a portion of her essay:

> I came back to Bates the next day and went to talk to the professor. The grade was correct. I had dug myself a hole in the class early on, and I failed the final. I was devastated. I was one credit short of graduating with my class. My family was supposed to be flying in for the ceremony, and I wasn't going to be in it. I wasn't even going to be allowed to walk with the class . . .
>
> I commuted to Bates three times a week second semester while continuing to work at a local ski area. After getting a 98 on the first test, I felt both elated and depressed at the same time. One part of me was ecstatic that I did so well, while the other part of me cursed myself for not doing the work the first time around. I ended up with a B for the course, and a year later I found myself on the graduation platform.
>
> Everyone should be able to experience this kind of joy and accomplishment. I am certain you will have similar feelings at your high school graduation. Just remember, never give up. To give up would be to rob yourself of an opportunity to excel. No person can be perfect, but you can always strive to be your best and LEARN from your blunders and mishaps. Capitalize on your mistakes. Live in the present, move on from the past. Now I KNOW that's what life is all about.

Thanks to Colleen, Jack, and the other visitors, my students begin to discover there is no one right way to work or live a life. Indeed, they get an-

Who am I?

Business Consultant—like a doctor except for business
Work mostly with very large companies
Have been working here for over one year to help mill
Live in New York—commute home on weekends
Have a radio show on business

Why my work is important:

Cost effective
Current skills, sometimes even set the trends in business
Help companies in time of need—ensure long term viability

My education:

Technical—Mechanical Engineering
Social—The-ologies

Your class:

Who is planning on going to college?
What careers?
Thoughts on employment after school—have you been following trends?
Any entrepreneurs? Joey K., 14 year old exec. of his own computer company
Any ideas on why entrepreneurs are so important to the future of our country?

The future:

Let's talk about the future in terms of three things:

1. Changing markets for our companies
   Global arena
   Fierce competition
   Changes in business will ultimately lead to cultural changes in USA—will you be ready?
2. Social aspect of the future companies
   Virtual companies—exits as a concept, but very real in what they can do
   More specialists because of less structure
   You will hold many jobs throughout your career
   You will embrace many types of employment—full time, part time, contract, etc.
3. Technology will play a key role in how a business runs and services its customers
   You must be technically capable
   You will use technology every day in the course of conducting business

Themes for future success:

Education is essential
Learning is a lifelong process
Flexibility is critical
Specialized skills are everything
Remain open to new ideas/thoughts

Use intellect to solve problems
Must be adaptable to changes
Must be technically competent
Ethnocentricity is deadly
Become a global citizen—no blinders

Figure 1–1. Jack Jacchino's Life Work Outline

other glimpse of the world beyond Room 109. The idea for this initial theme came to me after reading Donald Hall's glorious memoir, *Life Work* (Beacon Press 1993), written during the poet's battle with cancer. I knew immediately this theme would support my building toward (a.k.a. instructional scaffolding) the students' end-of-year independent study projects.

In all of this I have a number of roles, from organizer to mediator to cheerleader. Perhaps my most important work is to blend into classroom discussions. I work hard at staying in the wings, keeping my comments to a minimum. A lot of what I have to say is delivered in class letters. Parts of these stream-of-consciousness letters serve as the genesis of our discussions; other parts make good subjects for journal entries or essays due for their portfolios.

I work with my students before our visitors begin arriving. I speak extensively about being a good audience member through listening and questioning.

"Keep eye contact with the speaker," I say. "Nod your head once in a while, especially when our guest is looking at you. Don't be afraid to smile, too!" Heads begin nodding and smiles appear. *They really do want to please.*

"But what if they're boring?" asks Chad, who seems to exist for the other side of most issues.

"Chad raises a good point." I attempt to assuage his attack. "Most of the time, the more the audience supports the speaker, the better the speaker's presentation."

"Sheesh," he wheezes, rolling his eyes white.

He begins carrying on as Chad often does. This day, however, I turn my head downward toward my journal. Then, ignoring his harangue, I look over at Melissa and whisper a couple of words.

"Mr. Kent! You're not listening," he gripes.

I look up and smirk. *Exactly.* Chad lowers his head by degrees. I got him, and he knows it.

The kids smile as we continue talking about how to develop appropriate questions for our guests—boring or not.

The following is a list of questions we came up with for our Life Work visitors:

What do you do on your typical day?

How did you prepare for this occupation?

What's the best part of this job?

What's the worst?

Do you know what the job market is for this job?

What opportunities for advancement are there in this job?

What's the average starting pay?

What are the qualifications needed for this job?

What personal characteristics does someone need to be successful in this job?

Would you go into this field again? If not, why? What might you like to do instead?

What subjects in high school should we take if we're interested in this career?

What general advice do you have for someone entering this field?

Portfolios as Life Work vehicles

Having students develop portfolios goes hand-in-hand with the first-quarter theme of Life Work. These books are highly individualized creations that allow students the autonomy of the world beyond school. Businesspeople are especially impressed when they review our portfolios. Not only do they represent a great deal of work, but these student collections require plenty of independent decision making, a fine forerunner to the freedom my students will experience during their fourth-quarter independent studies.

Since Room 109 is a heterogeneous, multiaged, portfolio-based English classroom, my student colleagues produce a myriad of different papers and projects by the end of the eight- or nine-week quarter. I have a base number of inclusions for their portfolios:

- Three formal papers (a variety of genre encouraged), highly drafted, 600–1000 words long with all drafts included, signed and dated by your editor
- Two informal papers, revised once, 600–1000 words, draft included
- Forty-eight 1-page journal entries of approximately 150 words each
- Five books read
- Handouts and notes taken
- Three to five art projects and/or presentations over books or themes
- A copy of the reflection from the previous quarter
- *Keeper* letter (parent, guardian, or trusted adult letter response to the student's portfolio)

The work the students create reflects the theme or experience of the quarter—in this instance, we focused on Life Work, which included the talks by outside guests and discussions on the theme of money. Since my student colleagues have distinct differences as readers, writers, and thinkers, not to mention a variety of interests, each portfolio is unique.

At the end of each quarter in my portfolio letters, I attempt to connect to students on a number of levels. As an English language arts teacher, I do the best I can to touch upon their reading, writing, speaking, listening, performing, observing, and all the rest of their English "stuff." I also focus on the person and their futures.

My thinking in developing a teaching practice based on portfolio development stems from my own experience as a portfolio keeper at Middlebury College's Bread Loaf School of English. There, guided academic freedom helped my learning self take flight. There, too, I heard my teacher, the late James Britton, utter the words that have ever since adorned my classroom wall, leaving an indelible mark on my belief system as a teacher:

Being told is the opposite of finding out.

Surely, Mr. Britton's words represent the spirit of independent study projects.

From Maine to Alaska: Little People Pen Pals

"We did this in fourth grade," whispers Kelly.

Agreed. This is not a novel idea. (Heck, neither is bringing in outside speakers to talk about their careers.) Nevertheless, being pen pals helps my students consider life beyond our classroom while creating authentic writing and learning opportunities.

In an E-mail exchange, my Alaskan friend Suzie Cary and I decided our classes would share letters. As with everything Suzie touches, this small project turned into much more. Soon, state flags and Maine blueberry pins, calendars and candy canes, multicolored maple leaves and letters—always letters—began flying back and forth between her first graders and my high schoolers.

Throughout the year, my students learn about writing for a specific audience. In class they reminisce about their own elementary school experiences, from *Sesame Street* to a favorite superhero. Through these shared memories, my students connect and make meaning of their own experiences while attempting to think as six-year-olds.

"What do you think they'd like to hear about?" asks Robin.

"I was just writing the word *relationships*," says Dustin. "Is that too big of a word?"

"I've got a brother in the first grade," laughs Laura. "The other day he said, 'Evidently, you're confused about this issue.' Can you believe it?"

They're on their way. Being responsive to an audience helps these young writers determine the specifics of diction, theme, and point of view. But they're not thinking about this. They just want to communicate clearly with these little people. Prompted by the writing of these Alaskan first graders, Nathan looked closely at his own reading history in a journal. The following is a small section:

I never read, I didn't like it. My 4th grade teacher Mrs. Petrie gave me a book. She said the boy in this story reminds me of you. I couldn't wait to read it. That's when I realized the names and people in the stories could be me or some friends. I like to read now but only certain stuff. Funny how I remembered that from reading these little kid letters.

The scaffolding provided by this pen pal experience helped Nathan and others mature as readers and writers. These conversations and journal entries are the by-products of a constructivist activity that is centered around authentic student experience and reflection on the experience, which is the mantra of my classroom philosophy:

EXPERIENCE + REFLECTION ON EXPERIENCE = LEARNING

As for Suzie's students? She writes:

The exchange is a wonderful memory. The letters, cards, pins, a license plate, and large posters of your students made a lasting impression. We were able to extend beyond writing to geography (Where the heck is Maine, anyway? One child connected Rumford with an uncle in Portland); science (Remember the maple leaves?); and math (Just how many students does Mr. Kent teach? If Mr. Kent sends 30 pins to my class of 24, how many pins are left over?). The anticipation of packages and letters, for first graders, was a great motivator! In return, I remember the children eager to send letters and other items back to their friends in Maine just so they could share about themselves and their lives in Juneau. What fun!

The simple act of sharing letters with first graders a few thousand miles away helped my students learn more about their writing selves and inched us toward the independent study projects door.

From Maine to China:
University Pen Pals

It is persons least like ourselves who often teach us most about ourselves. They challenge us to examine what we have uncritically assumed to be true and raise our eyes to wider horizons.

James O. Freedman,
President
Dartmouth College, May
17, 1991

As a classroom teacher, I alone can not sustain my students' interest day in and day out. I am neither entertainer nor sage, just a guy trying to connect with over one hundred teenagers. In the younger grades, teachers spend their days "connecting play and outside events" (Paley 1986). In secondary school, I must develop a series of opportunities and experiences for my students that provide glimpses of themselves—their emerging adult selves—in the outside world.

This became clearer to me after a letter exchange with students from a large university in China. This sharing of words and ideas, which took place just after the Tiananmen Square protests, moved my student colleagues to think about culture. We also began discussions on the ethnocentric ways of Americans. By using these letters as focal points, our classroom discussions grew in worldly ways. And this from a group of rural Maine kids, the majority of whom have traveled only as far as Boston.

The university letters were carried secretly out of China by various friends and acquaintances of an American teacher working at the university on a scholarship. Portions of the teacher's cover letter and its postscript jolted our class conversations into overdrive: "Please ask the students not to make direct comments about communism. Their letters will be censored and political comments may be problematic for their pen pals."

The American teacher's warnings and the clandestine mailings coupled with the elegant handwriting and poetic words of our Chinese pen pals taught my students lessons while raising "our eyes to wider horizons." Each student letter introduced new strands to the conversation. Many segments, read aloud by my incredulous teenagers, brought a series of "no ways" and furrowed brows. Here are four such segments:

> Shanghai is said to be the biggest city of China. It's so important to China that it is, so to speak, the supporter of the whole nation. But to tell you the truth, it's public service isn't the most convenient in China, especially as far as the transportation system is concerned. Could you image how many people there are on one bus during rush hour? Someone stated that there were 12 persons' feet on the $1m^2$ surface.

In class, six of my kids balanced precariously in a square meter I had taped off on the floor. I told them about the jobs some older Chinese worked. Their sole job is to shove people into the buses—to pack them in so the doors will shut.

> Nowadays, my country have a new policy for students, and going to America for further study becomes impossible. So I'm sorry for being un-

able to meet you. If you have chance to visit Shanghai I wish I could see you and show you around.

Even though the possibility of overseas travel for most of my students seems as remote as playing second base for the Red Sox, they still feel the sting of confinement from these words. To bring the feeling closer to home, I suggest not being able to day-trip from our town across the nearby Canadian border for snow mobiling or fishing.

Our government people are shits.

After the laughter subsided, I explained the very real possibility of jail time for such a comment. The ensuing discussion went from flag burning to protecting the rights of neo-Nazis here in the USA. Other lines from letters helped each of us see more clearly the subtle differences between China and America.

I deeply love my parents and sister though I never say "I love you" to them. Such expression is often used between lovers. We Chinese seldom express our feelings directly but it doesn't follow that we don't know other's hearts. We are accustomed to feeling love, affection and friendship from people's actions, words, even expressions on face. Our culture is quite different from yours, isn't it?

How my students grow from these letters

"When we are curious about a child's words and our responses to those words, the child feels respected. The child *is* respected" (Paley 1986). Though Chicago kindergarten teacher Vivian Gussin Paley applied these words to a teacher's role, I view the words of people beyond our classroom as appendages of the teacher and the curriculum. Both sets of letters from away created whole-world learning opportunities for my students. Even more, my students grew to understand that they were being listened to and respected by brilliant Chinese doctoral students. In essence, these young Mainers were teaching lessons in American culture and the English language.

When the Chinese students misinterpreted some of the American kids' stories, these misunderstandings helped create a deeper awareness of language and custom. Our classroom conversations ran the gamut from How does culture affect meaning and understanding? to What exactly is funny in another country?

As a result of the Chinese pen pal experience, a number of students selected such books as *Encounters with Chinese Writers* by Annie Dillard and *The Woman Warrior* by Maxine Hong Kingston. With both the personal letters and the books in hand, they made the necessary whole world connection between literature and life. Furthermore, these young readers became more thoughtful of other cultures. All of this reinforced the foundation of experience that would allow them to venture with confidence beyond our classroom.

Using E-mail to Connect and See Beyond

Much like the pen pal experience, connecting past and present students via E-mail has an enriching effect on everyone and helps kids see that there is a light at the end of the high school tunnel.

While I was reading Katey's reflection from third quarter she mentioned considering an ISP on dance. I immediately dashed off an E-mail to Josie, a former student studying at Boston's Emerson College, a performing arts school. Josie immediately wrote to Katey.

Hey Katey!
Mr. Kent tells me that you are interested in doing an independent study on dance for his class. Do you have any thoughts on your project so far? Last year I did one that focused on Modern dance (which I had never studied until this year) and Gender issues within the dance movement. It's a lot of fun to experiment with different styles on your own, and not in the studio. There is so much to learn about. I am discovering this now even though I am only two weeks into class here at Emerson College. If you would like some advice on your project or anything, I would be happy to help. Josie

Hi!
I think that maybe ballet is what I am going to do. You gave me some good ideas about how I could do it in your last note. This year in my dance class, me and Teatra have made up our own dance to "Titanic" and are going to be performing it in the show. And, we made up another ballet solo for me to do also. So, maybe I could do some of those for the class, and show how we choreographed some stuff of our own? I probably could do some of the papers and projects you suggested, too. Well, I have to get back to psychology. I will talk to you later. Bye and Thanks! Katey

Josie's connection to Katey helped her move forward with her ISP on dance at the end of the year. Josie gave Katey the confidence to bring her love of dance into the classroom.

Chad is a senior student who is interested in pursuing a career in medicine. His contact is Matthew, who spent four years at the University of Pennsylvania in pre-med. Since I did not have Matthew's E-mail address, Chad had to touch base with Matt's parents. Phoning was one more solid life experience.

Typically, I don't hook up present students with past students just for the sake of chatting back and forth. There must be a real purpose driving the connection. The following are parts of the first couple of E-mails:

> Matt,
>
> When I spoke with your mother on the phone about the email address she mentioned that you did not know who I am, which makes sense considering . . . well . . . you don't :) I am a senior at Mountain Valley and I'm doing an independent study in Rich Kent's Writing Center class. He is the person who gave me your name to try to get in contact with. The project has to do with career exploration in the medical field. I understand that you have been accepted into medical school and what I was hoping is that I would be able to start up a semi-regular email correspondence with you. Chad W.
>
> PS I am curious, what is it that you are doing right now? Someone mentioned that you are doing some type of research. I would be interested to hear about it if you get the time. Thanks again.

> Dear Chad,
>
> Yep, sounds good to me. May as well use the miracle of email for something productive now and then. In answer to your question, I work in a molecular biology lab in the Bio dept. of U. of Pennsylvania, in Philly. We work on "the role of gap junctions in development" which sounds pretty wacky. Gap junctions allow cells next to each other to 'talk' to each other through very small channels. Small molecules such as ions and metabolites can pass through the junctions. Cells connected in this way are said to be 'coupled'. Some groups of cells in developing embryos are coupled in 'domains' that seem to be important to the developing fetus. We use mice to study the role of gap junctions. If you want more specific details I'd be happy to send you literature or stuff like that. To tell you the truth, I'm a little tired of the "academia" game, that is, always depending on the organizations such as the government to give money for research. Academics is like a weird little world unto itself. But it's kinda fun for the same reasons. It really is like a big game. Of course, I don't have to worry about this stuff directly as I'm a technician. Adios, Matt

Chad provides a reflective opportunity for Matthew, who is seven years out of high school. These E-mails supply a catalyst that allows and encourages Matthew to connect with his own past by listening and responding to this high schooler's questions. This is a chance to take inventory of his life's journey from high school, through college, and on to three years of research assistant work in a laboratory. All of this ushers Matthew to the point of looking yet again at his ultimate goal of becoming a doctor.

Chad immediately realizes the effect this sharing has on him. He's chatting on E-mail with someone other than a buddy from school. He's accomplishing real work—researching pre-med, seeking advice, looking for inroads—while connecting and imagining his future self through another's experiences. Matt offers a midpoint view of the journey to medical practice.

During the first few E-mail exchanges, Chad makes a connection to Matthew's research of "the role of gap junctions in development."

> Wow, that AP Bio last year paid off. I actually understand exactly what you are doing in your research. It seems quite interesting and I would love to have some more info on it if you get a second.

Some of Chad's questions help him with the practical issues of his pre-med and medical school future: " . . . how is it that you came to be a part of this research?" I could hear the wheels turning as Chad started formulating the map of his own medical school journey. Matthew's experiences in the laboratory show Chad that going to medical school might not be a straight shot. It's not necessarily four years of undergraduate school, four years of medical school, internship, residency, and a lucrative practice. As with many careers, the road to doctoring may have forks, detours, or dead-ends. All along these roads, the student will be faced with a variety of choices. FYI: Matthew is now in medical school, and Chad is in pre-med.

Using Our School Community as a Research Project

What better way to involve students in authentic learning and research than by having them look closely at their own school, which is to say, their own community? One project we undertook quite a few years ago focused on re-thinking (restructuring) our school's time schedule from a seven-period day to a block schedule of ninety-minute periods. I shared sections of education books I had been reading. We spoke about radical changes in schooling across the country. As a result, the students approached the principal with individual letters concerning the changes they desired. Here is an example by Hannah:

> Dear Mr. Rowe,
> Anger is the only word that can describe my feelings. I can't believe that I have spent thirteen years in school and I'm still not ready for what the real world has to offer. If any other feeling comes close to anger, it is shame. I'm

ashamed because I didn't try to do something sooner. I'm also ashamed of the fact that I remained satisfied with my education for so long.

The first step toward change is awareness. So many people believe that our educational system is great, or at least as good as it can get. Maybe we, as students, need to write letters to anyone and everyone to make them aware of the system's failure. I would be more than willing to do this if you thought that it might help to set the wheels in motion.

A form of the Copernican Plan has been found most favorable among the students in Mr. Kent's class. Students need more time to focus on one particular subject area, rather than trying to absorb six or seven subject areas per day.

Why don't school officials notice that the sheltered life of high school does not prepare students for what lies ahead? In order to function as adults, we must first be taught and treated like adults.

I hope you'll agree to help us change the system.

Sincerely,
Hannah

Our principal, Mr. Rowe, responded to the students' letters with enthusiasm and support.

TO: Room 109 Students
FR: T. E. R.
RE: "Operation Education"
Thank you very much for your ideas and plans for the five-day trial. You have my 100% cooperation. Now there needs to be a game plan of action, one that takes into account all aspects of the week. SUGGESTIONS: NOT NECESSARILY IN THE RIGHT ORDER.

1. Meet with all teachers and present plan. (Remember, it won't work unless teachers support it.)
2. Meet with curriculum committee so that they will be well enough informed to present to the school board.
3. Should have dates set and an evaluation form in place.
4. Should be present for moral support when presented to board.
5. Individual teachers should be talked with before presentation to whole faculty. The more individuals you have in your camp, the easier to convince the "whole."

Mr. Rowe's letter fired up my students. Armed with their newfound knowledge and freshly copied materials about block scheduling, they trucked off through the school with the principal's blessings to talk with each member of the staff and ask for a written comment.

When the students returned, they brought a mixed bag of responses from the high school staff. I'd never seen quite this much focused energy from my Period Four students. I attribute their enthusiasm and energy to doing real work of the world—their world. The discussions with staff members provided enough material for a full range of lively discussions in class.

Next, these young researchers interviewed students throughout the school. Amidst some rather volatile observations were those that revealed genuine thoughtfulness. A common theme emerged, one that did not surprise any of us. In the end the message rang clear: The students wanted and needed a change.

Our next step, a half-day inservice for the staff led by my students, made me anxious. The kids' response to my suggestions to "Be polite and don't act like know-it-alls" made me smile: "Don't worry, Mr. Kent. We won't embarrass you."

And they didn't. The students sat casually at the base of our tiered lecture hall. Fifty-five members of the faculty and staff listened as the students talked about learning styles, lecture courses, and teaching. They discussed the need for more time in the classroom to allow for immersion. The passion in the voices of these senior students showed me that they cared about their school.

This kind of research helped my students and me feel useful and productive. The work we did affected our own community, and the results made a difference: Mountain Valley High School moved from a traditional forty-three minute, seven-period day to a block schedule of ninety-minute periods. Relevance is the key to success in any work we undertake in or out of the classroom.

Other In-School Experiences in Preparation for Escape

Activities such as our Alaskan letter exchange help students experience authentic, whole-world moments without leaving school. Many other in-class projects we have undertaken have connected my students with the outside world and have helped them prepare for ISP.

Providing editing services for the younger grades

My students work with students from the younger grades during the course of the year. Their stories, essays, and poems arrive via interoffice mail, and we write letters back in reaction to the young writers' work. Sometimes, the young authors come visit us at the high school to share their final products. Imagine being in the seventh grade and having a high school senior respond to your short story. Listen to a paragraph from Jen's response to Alicia:

> I enjoyed your short story, "The Calm and Peaceful Night." I thought that you
> really showed the reader the strong and loving relationship between the grand-

father and his grandson. I liked how you used the grizzly bear to describe the grandfather. Your words gave me a good picture of him, and they made me feel that if I were to see him out on a street that I would know who he was.

Hosting Elementary School Children

Each year my English colleague, Dorothy Peters, has her tenth-grade students compose holiday stories for children. In December, just before the winter vacation, long lines of little people tiptoe through the high school hallways on their way to listen to stories. Along with the readings, the kids enjoy cookies and milk. Not only does this project engage Mrs. Peters' students in writing for a specific audience, but they must also communicate with the little guys. This is a great project for young and not-so young students.

Volunteering in the Writing Center (math center or learning center)

The Writing Center at our school, housed in the media center and in Room 109, offers an opportunity for my students to work as editors for the school community at large. Although the media center director is on duty, there is no teacher overseeing the moment-by-moment interchanges of editors and clients. Student editors are in charge of the time as they work with a wide variety of students from throughout the school. Working in the center is a solid whole-world activity.

I have visited a number of high school learning centers. They are places of high energy where learning takes center stage as students from throughout the school receive academic assistance from peers or teachers. Peer tutors can benefit by this excellent opportunity to teach others. To be sure, we truly learn a subject once we become teachers of it.

Inviting university students and teachers to visit

Each year we invite students and teachers from one or more university classes to visit Room 109 to learn more about portfolios. Their full range of questions as well as their seriousness elevates my student colleagues' thinking and behavior. In this case, these high school kids are the teachers for students older than themselves, so they must adjust their communication and presentation skills accordingly.

Utilizing classroom volunteers

My friend and French teaching colleague, Anne Wood, has two adult volunteers, Frances and Carla, who grace her classroom. Frances is a seventy-five-year-old woman with a French Canadian heritage. Her charming presence helps Ms. Wood's fifteen-year-olds in many ways, not the least of which is learning to speak French. Carla is from France. She, too, helps students by offering individualized attention. As Ms. Wood says, "Their generous visits result in enriched language opportunities, warm personal communication, and new levels of confidence for my students."

This year we have a young exchange student from France. Frequently, Anne will invite Yvon into her class to help her students' pronunciation. Even though sixteen-year old Yvon is there to correct his new friends' speaking, the difference a young person from another culture makes in a classroom and a school can be important. Clearly, bringing people in from outside the school culture broadens my student's understanding of subject and, in a real way, themselves.

Interviewing members of the high school staff and student body

My students have interviewed the sixty or more adults in this school as well as members of the student body, for a variety of purposes (e.g., block scheduling). From putting together a list of favorite books to asking opinions on school-related issues, working with adults one-on-one is a practical, whole-world experience.

Utilizing students as research assistants

I include my students in as much of my research work as possible. They perform Internet searches, interview *keepers* (a parent, guardian, or trusted adult), and respond to inquiries from other schools. I've had students interview past and present students about their experiences in Room 109 to help me come to know more about my practice. Over the past couple of years, I have asked veteran students to review certain aspects of 109's curriculum and write their observations and suggestions. Often, my present students collaborate on their research projects with former 109ers who are in college—one more solid connection to the outside world.

Posting book suggestions on our conference site

"Books of 109" is a site on our district's computer network. Students post a short comment about a book they've read; beginning this year they posted an explanation of their ISP. All of my students are required to post at least one book per quarter. Students from all of my classes (plus anyone who wants to look in on the bulletin board) have access to this site. The wide audience for these blurbs adds to the importance and the authenticity of the experience.

Tyla Giroux	2K A Woman's Worth	02/12	02:13 PM
James McLean	1K This Boy's Life	02/12	10:35 AM
Jami Blouin	2K Ryan White Story	02/12	10:20 AM

Sandra Capitan	1K The Yellow Wallpaper	02/12	10:08 AM
Seth Hoyt	2K Stephen Hawking	02/12	09:15 AM
David Gallagher	2K The Color Purple	02/11	02:20 PM
Amy Bernard	1K Little Women	02/11	02:06 PM
Zane Sjoberg	2K To Renew America	02/11	12:20 PM
Kevin Estes	1K Education of Little Tree	02/11	11:15 AM
Jessica Glover	1K Annie Frank	02/11	09:17 AM

Printed by: **<your name here>**   Tuesday, February 11   11:15 AM
Title: **Education of Little Tree**   Page 1 of 1

Tuesday, February 11   11:15 AM
Books of 109 Item
From: Kevin Estes
Subject: Education of Little Tree
To: Books of 109

A beautifully simplistic account of a young Cherokee boy raised by his grandparents in the mountains during the 1930s. He learns from his grandparents the ways of the mountain and the world around him. This autobiographical story ignites almost every human emotion possible. It's deeply moving. I strongly recommend this book to anyone who is even remotely human.

Exchanging E-mail

The miracle of electronic mail certainly creates innumerable opportunities for students to connect with schools, organizations, and others. On various teacher listservs I find teachers from around the world who want to have E-mail exchanges with students. These conversations help my students think globally.

We have just recently begun sharing essays for editing with former students and with on-line college writing centers.

Publishing a class newspaper

Although *The 109 Voice* had a short run of it, the experience for my students and me enriched our understanding of difference. The issues presented in *The 109 Voice* created too much controversy for our moderately conservative, mill-town high school. The response to the newspaper brought on incredible discussion and argument among students and staff. It was wonderful. However, the editors tread on sacred ground too often and the superintendent of schools ordered its dismantling. As soon as things calm down around here, I'm sure we'll give a classroom newspaper another shot.

Utilizing student assistants

Similar to the research assistants, student assistants work for teachers in our building and receive credit. The brainchild of my English chair, Pete St. John, student assistants perform everything from secretarial work to research. This is a good opportunity for students who are thinking about working in the business field or the teaching field to learn more about how these worlds operate.

Engaging student workers

Students with special talents or needs are given opportunities to broaden their skills. A number of our computer "techies" work with the district's computer coordinator. They have an opportunity to work throughout the district gaining experience in computers and relating to a diverse group of people. These students troubleshoot, install software, teach students and staff, and make repairs.

Some of our special needs students help our custodial workers and groundskeepers. Sometimes special students deliver televisions and VCRs for our media center. Such work experiences help socialize these young people while boosting their self-confidence.

Volunteering as a spokesperson on parent/guardian—teacher night

When *keepers* visit our high school to chat with teachers about their kids, I solicit student volunteers as spokespersons for Room 109. Sixteen to twenty-four students enjoy the experience—two to three students for each hour of the eight-hour afternoon and evening. Each team of students staffs the hallway outside our classroom. They discuss portfolios, hand out Writing Center brochures, point out various activities in the photographs displayed, and show off the many student projects lining the hall. I give the spokespersons a talk about how to work the hallway. They always have fun stories to tell after their stint. This activity is not only a valuable experience for these teenagers, but is a fine public relations effort for my practice.

Performing in school plays and musicals

I award extra credit for those students who join school productions. From stage hand to star, this experience is absolutely enriching. I also offer extra consideration to those 109ers who attend school productions, congratulate the performers, directors, and workers, and then write reactions to what they experienced.

Responding to student portfolios

On two consecutive weekends at the end of each quarter, student volunteers from Room 109 come in to read and respond to portfolios. On these Saturday and Sunday mornings, they read and respond to three portfolios from my other classes. Responding to students they don't know or know only slightly, aids them in many whole-world ways, one of which is learning to write comments and reactions with tact.

Operating a school store

We used to have a school store at Mountain Valley High School. The room is now a storage area where staff members copy, bind, and laminate. However, our school's life skills class still grows flowers in the springtime and sells them for Mother's Day. This experience offers opportunities for them to learn directly about holding down a job and working with the public.

Creating multimedia packages and Web pages

Creating Web pages or multimedia packages gives the author an opportunity to think about a large, diverse audience. Working in collaboration with the computer coordinator of a nearby elementary school, David developed a multimedia package on the history of his town. Together they presented their work during a town gathering. Three computer literate members of Room 109 spent an entire quarter developing a multimedia package showing the ins and outs of Room 109. Undeniably, the "infosphere" offers our students a universe of in-school opportunities.

Inviting guests from outside the school world

After studying the history of ski racing in our town, Cara invited a former Olympic skier to speak to class. During show 'n' tell, Jenn brought in her mom, Jamie his nephew, and Kristin a lamb. When we study "What it is to be a woman" and "What it is to be a man," the doors swing open to a variety of community folks who enjoy young people. As with the Life Work visitors, classroom volunteers, and elementary school guests, the more contact with a variety of people, the better.

Volunteering in the life skills room

A number of 109ers enjoy working with students in our life skills room. The experience of dealing with special needs children helps my students not only learn to accept difference but to think critically in developing ways to work with a variety of learners.

Working as a class in different parts of the school

Moving our class to the auditorium, the bandroom, the biology laboratories, the vocational area, the gymnasium, the lecture hall, the computer room, the media center, or the principal's conference room creates new learning opportunities. Heck, just walking down the school's corridors can be a learning experience. Next time students have plays to perform or a speech to present, make arrangements to go to a different venue. This change of surroundings will be refreshing and can offer teaching moments quite unlike those your own classroom affords.

Stage 109: Preparing Students for ISP Interviews and Conversations

All through the school year I work to come up with different experiences to help my students learn to communicate more effectively. They deliver a variety of projects in front of their classmates, enter into countless classroom discussions, interview elderly people, visit elementary schools, talk to class guests, and survey the school community. During third quarter I take the communication lesson to the next level, preparing for out-of-school ISP work. This quarter, called Stage 109, is a playful and meaningful time. Kids come back year after year to tell me how important it was for them to address these communication issues, especially in a nonthreatening manner.

For this unit I arrange my small classroom so there's a stage at one end. I'd love to have risers—heck, I'd like to have a phone, the Internet, and a whole lot of other things—however, we do with what we have, and borrow the rest. The following describes the various performances 109 students enjoy through the quarter.

- Introductions—I have my students pretend they are introducing themselves to a group of twenty-five high school students from different towns. They give their names, school, hometown, and one or two small bits of information about themselves. Part of the activity asks students to create a purpose for the student gathering. For example, one student might be at a meeting of the Abused Women's Advocacy Project; another meeting might be for all-state soccer players.

    My simple directions: stand up and face the entire group (unless seated in a circle); attempt to look all around the group; be yourself; don't try to be funny; don't squirm or wiggle with hands or feet; speak loudly and clearly. Smile!
- Show 'n' tell—In one to two minutes, my students show something to the class and tell us something about it. The difference from elementary school? Be totally organized and well practiced. The show 'n' tell presentation should have a beginning, a middle, and an ending. Students must exhibit confidence and work to look around at the entire audience.
- Read or recite a poem—I ask my students to select a poem or song lyrics that they enjoy. They practice the piece to the point where they are looking up and around at the audience more than at the book or paper. This does not have to be a dramatic reading, but if students choose to do one, great! Some people even dress up for their part.

- Read from a novel, essay, or screenplay—Following the general guidelines of the poem reading above, my students read for two to three minutes. Once again, this does not have to be a dramatic reading; however, if they're so inclined, they may dress up and have a blast.
- Improvisations—I place students, in small groups to begin with, into a number of different scenes. Some of my favorite improvs include: Two teenagers talking about a mutual friend who has been stealing things from people; two aghast teenage siblings talking about their parents and how they've begun holding hands and, once in a while, kissing each other on the cheek *in public.*

    I also have grab bags of seventy-five common items (e.g., ring, wooden box, magic wand) for improvisation tools. Students take out a bag, open it, and make something up about the item or act with it. These improvs are hilarious.
- Demonstration—In three to five minutes, demonstrate a talent or a skill. As with the other performances, students must make sure the presentation is highly organized, simple to follow, and has a beginning, a middle, and an ending. Eye contact and confidence are crucial. Students have demonstrated everything from yoga to waxing skis.
- Interviews—I will either bring each student to the front of the class and chat with her or him, or I will come up with a series of interview questions and have students interview one another in front of the class. The questions will be much like those addressed in college entrance interviews or job interviews.
- Miniplay or skit—In five to ten minutes with a small group of two to four people, present a scene from a play, movie, or television show. You may also write a script of your own. Have costumes and some sort of set. Students in the past have done everything from *Hamlet* to *Saturday Night Live!* skits.

An Aside: A Note on the Constructivist Nature of Room 109

Many would call my classroom approach a constructivist pedagogy, where I "encourage and accept student autonomy, where raw data and primary sources (rather than textbooks) are used in investigations, where student thinking drives the lessons, and where dialogue, inquiry, and puzzlement are valued" (Brooks and Brooks 1993, viii). I agree.

The following, from *In Search of Understanding: The Case for Constructivist Classrooms* (Brooks and Brooks 1993, 17) helps clarify my understanding of constructivism and presents a clearer view of what we're doing in Room 109:

Traditional Classrooms	**Constructivist Classrooms**
Curriculum is presented part to whole, with emphasis on basic skills.	Curriculum is presented whole to part with emphasis on big concepts.

Strict adherence to fixed curriculum is highly valued.	Pursuit of student questions is highly valued.
Curriculum activities rely heavily on textbooks and workbooks.	Curriculum activities rely heavily on primary sources of data and manipulative material.
Students are viewed as "blank slates" onto which information is etched by the teacher.	Students are viewed as thinkers with emerging theories about the world.
Teachers generally behave in a didactic manner, disseminating information to students.	Teachers generally behave in an interactive manner, mediating the environment for students
Teachers seek the correct answer to validate student learning.	Teachers seek the students' point of view in order to understand students' present conceptions for use in subsequent lessons.
Assessment of student learning is viewed as separate from teaching and occurs almost entirely through testing.	Assessment of student learning is interwoven with teaching and occurs through teacher observations of students at work and through exhibitions and portfolios.
Students primarily work alone.	Students primarily work in groups.

Constructivism is a beautifully respectful statement about knowledge and learning. Surely, this philosophy touches James Britton's thinking about the "deinstitutionalization and depedagogicalization of the classroom" (1991). Juxtaposing the fundamental principles of constructivism and one's classroom practices begins the exhilarating process of reinventing what we do and how we do it. This is the life of a teacher-researcher: the continual observation, questioning, and reflection of one's practice in order to be more responsive to individual students.

As I consider my day-to-day role in the classroom and attempt to balance my work as advisor, coach, or mentor, I am ushered to new levels of thought concerning my responsibilities. Lev Vygotsky might say that in Room 109 I am dancing in the *zone of proximal development,* "that zone being the difference between what a learner can do independently and what he or she can do with various kinds of support" (Hillocks 1995). In my eyes, this is teaching.

2

Escaping: Out-of-School Projects

Now we're ready to escape. Whether for short jaunts or daylong adventures, my students need experiences beyond the schoolhouse walls.

During those years when money is not available for school buses, we work within walking distance of our school. Sometimes we solicit *keepers* (a parent, guardian, or trusted adult) to drive. Or, if the students gain permission from their *keepers*, the school office, and me, they may use their personal cars to leave school to tutor in the elementary schools, research an issue at a university, or visit a business, state agency, and so on. However this happens— via school bus, foot, or personal cars—these escapes are precursors to their last-quarter independent studies. Indeed, these experiences give my students a chance to enjoy the freedom and decision making that accompany such autonomy.

Scotty's Mountain: Stepping Out of the Schoolhouse Door

One of my favorite escapes is right in the backyard of our high school, where the remnants of a 1950s ski area lay virtually undisturbed for all those who are ambitious and curious enough to look carefully.

I explain the task at hand to my students while we stand on the hillside meadow. Their jobs are to explore, to play, to rummage, to discover, and to re-port back on all that they have found. It is an observer's scavenger hunt; I ask that nothing be disturbed. "Just look. *Don't touch anything.*" Once admonished, they scurry up and down the mountainside announcing their discoveries.

"Look! This must have been where the ski tow was."

"I bet this stuff was part of a ski jump."

After an hour of hunting, we gather near the bottom of the hill and com-pare notes. Many of the kids have drawn pictures, mapped out sites, shim-mied up trees, or crawled into thickets. They're sweating, wired, and ready to get back to it. Here, in the browning grass of fall, they chatter like a class-

26

room of kindergartners returning from a weekend to discover that the little seeds in the Styrofoam cup have indeed sprouted green wings of life.

Dashing about on Scotty's Mountain my students learn the magic of discovery in heuristic moments suspended in a spirit of energy and hope. Times like this comprise some of the defining moments in my teaching and my life.

As always, some students remain quiet and out of touch here on the side of Scotty's Mountain. They gave up the hunt ten or fifteen minutes into the adventure, if they even tried at all. These students have lost the wonder and excitement of exploring. I think to myself, *Did they ever have it? What do I do with these young people?* And always, the answer lies in the hard and personal work of forming a relationship of trust through listening. This is the foundation of my teaching. Whether with kids who live in detention hall or with those who eat up AP courses like some people pop M&Ms, I listen, and I listen. This is never easy with one hundred or more students, and I can assure you I am not always successful.

Scotty's Projects

Once we leave Scotty's Mountain and return to the classroom, my role as teacher-advisor begins. Each student is to do something—a paper or a project—with this experience that will fulfill one or more of their portfolio requirements. It's their choice. Some of these teenagers have fantastic imaginations, and why not? They are our future inventors, actors, scientists, and explorers.

A few are in high gear instantly. They don't ask for my help; in fact, they don't want my help. They savor the freedom created by the absence of a teacher's prearranged, minute-by-minute curriculum or agenda. Some are immediately on the phone; others head to Joe Sassi, our media center director, to chat about a history book that might include photos of the old ski area. Still others truck down the hallway to Jeff Turnbull's classroom. A local historian, Mr. Turnbull will have "tons of stuff."

To those kids who sat in the shade on Scotty's chit-chatting about parties, this whole idea is "stupid." "This ain't English, Mr. Kent." Our conversations begin slowly and without threats. My feelings aren't hurt because they think this project is dumb. I have a job to do. I listen and pose questions that I hope will open up possibilities. Then, I leave them alone. They don't need to be told. They've heard it all over and over again. I'll give them a few days to think about it.

Within ten days, the first Scotty's projects begin to surface. Peter's dad supplies him with hundreds of feet of string. He and his buddy, Jacob, spend two class periods and two hours on a Sunday morning out on Scotty's, building a model of the old rope tow with the string. They've discovered a number of metal car wheels that were used to guide the rope up the mountain. Some of the wheels are still high in the trees; others have since fallen off, marking the path the skiers took to the top.

The two boys—who now call themselves "archaeological recon-structionists" (where they got this term I haven't the slightest)—bring us out to Scotty's and give us a talk on rope tows. We walk the mountain from base to summit following the string. They show us the cement slab at the bottom where the tow's engine rested. They point out each of the "towers" where the wheels hung. And finally, they show us the tow's turn-around point at the summit; the wheels have grown into the pine tree where they were attached. The boys' animated explanations and descriptions bring us to another time.

Back in class, Peter and Jacob entertain us with part of a black-and-white ski film borrowed from a local ski coach that includes scenes of a rope tow in action and people are dressed in 1940s ski attire. We howl at the outmoded gear, replete with wooden skis and old leather boots. The boys also collaborated on a three-by-four-foot scale drawing of Scotty's, which depicts the rope tow, the main slopes, the ski jumps, and the small shack at the base. They mounted the drawing on plywood and covered it with Plexiglas. Finally, each wrote an essay in journal form about the work they had accomplished. They served as each other's editors through four revisions. The essay also included a small section on the history of Scotty's Mountain.

In terms of multiple intelligence work, Peter and Jacob have run the gamut. Certainly, they have accomplished the language arts requisites of reading, writing, editing, speaking, and researching. They studied history, interviewed people, and made observations. They tested their math skills, kinesthetic adeptness, and artistic ability while having an enormously fun time. For young men who enjoy working with their hands and trucking about in the woods, this project scored big points.

Briah and Janel played with the idea of marketing Scotty's Mountain. From old home movies of Briah's parents skiing, they created a television commercial for the ski area. They composed a catchy script and selected music. Using a computer and freehand artwork, they produced a brochure for the ski area that included a map, advertisements for a variety of products from the 1950s, and ski prices.

The research that went into this brochure helped develop its authenticity. Briah and Janel interviewed a number of ski people here in town, including ski legend and former Olympian Chummy Broomhall.

Throughout our Scotty's Mountain adventure, students play with possibilities. Some write first-person narratives about their experiences while others, like Briah and Janel, research, interview, and explore. For my student colleagues who are blossoming scientists, the noninvasive archaeological dig of Scotty's Mountain is a godsend in English class. In each case, students work toward their own interests. If they falter or stall, I'm never too far away.

Other Out-of-School Projects

Needless to say, few schools have abandoned ski areas in their backyards. But, out-of-school opportunities for both full classes and individual students abound whether the school is in a rural area or on the city streets.

Some activities, such as readings of poetry and prose at colleges, libraries, or bookstores, offer my students a rich exposure to another level of literacy appreciation. The same happens with plays and lectures; any such event for these rural mill-town teenagers helps broaden their understanding and awareness of the world beyond school and beyond our hometown of seven thousand people.

- Abandoned cars—The car enthusiasts in my classroom relish the opportunity to head into the deep woods around our community to perform postmortems on "ancient cars" (e.g., from the 1930s and 1940s). It's a great weekend activity. Once they've gained permission from the land owner, they begin dissecting the car to identify its make, model, and year. Some ambitious students try to find who dumped the car here and why. In a couple of cases, that's proven embarrassing for some older folks in town. Many students approach garage mechanics for their expertise; some consult car books, magazines, or the Internet; others chat with grandparents or older neighbors. The result is a rich experience of researching, discussing, interviewing, photographing (or videoing), and presenting to the class. Similar experiences could be accomplished at city junkyards, I suspect.
- Old buildings—Bringing a class to an older building and then, as with the Scotty's adventure, sending them off to discover what they can is pure excitement. Planning with the building's superintendent or owners is crucial. Access to the library, historical society, or local folks will enhance the student's experience.
- Nature walks with journal books—Often, we'll truck out of school and across the street to sit near the Swift River and write. Frequently in the fall or spring of the year we wander into our poetry garden to read and respond to the poems posted among the trees.
- Museums—With the right instruction from the teacher, a trip to the museum can become a true adventure. In art museums, pictures can be related to literature read. In science or history museums, artifacts can remind students of classroom themes, films watched, or books read. The simple instruction in an art museum might be, "In the next hour find as many connections as possible to books you've read."

- Abandoned farmhouse cellars—nineteenth century farmhouse cellars are scattered around the hillsides in Maine. In *Room 109* (Kent 1997, 90), I describe the experience of three students who dig at the remains of one such farmhouse. Another one of my students, named Ryan, had the good fortune to dig at the site of his great-grandfather's nineteenth-century farm. This connection to his family's past affected Ryan profoundly and was evident when he presented the remnants of his great-granddad's life—a touching moment for all of us. Ryan is now enrolled in an archeology undergraduate program.
- College archeological dig sites—Some of my science and history buff students have gained permission from various colleges to hang out and even wield a shovel at a dig site. Contacting professors and making all the other arrangements themselves add to my students' base of whole-world experience. Recently, a yearlong dig took place on the banks of the Androscoggin River here in town.
- Mills, malls, city parks, old baseball stadiums, Army surplus stores, college campuses, ocean beaches, old forts, game preserves, national forests, railway stations, airports, and even funeral homes provide opportunities for student observation and/or exploration.

One good piece of advice that all veteran teachers have learned firsthand and often painfully: Adventures away from school must be well planned, and all of the necessary players must be informed. The purpose of the experience must be clearly stated for the student and the product of the adventure has to be identified. Furthermore, students should not just feel "like" an archeologist, they must "be and act" as archeologists. If this is the case, and I hope I don't sound overly naive saying this, students will more likely attack the experience with maturity. However, there's no such thing as a guarantee with teenagers.

Brainstorming out-of-school ideas

Coming up with out-of-school experiences for my students isn't difficult. Here's an example I conjured up in just fifteen minutes. This involves working as researchers on a college campus. Let's say during a study of gender issues someone asked, "What subjects in college are most popular among males and females?" As a result, we decide to investigate the male/female student makeup of various courses at a particular college. For example, how many women take math courses and how many men are in nursing. Naturally, we could simply ask the college officials, but there's much more to be learned and experienced by having students conduct the research themselves.

The experience would have my students working as quantitative researchers, where "the researcher's role is to (objectively) observe and measure" (Glesne and Peshkin 1992, 6). I'd probably ask them to sit outside the science building for an hour or so, and keep track of the number of men and women entering the building. I know it's far from the most reliable of research techniques, but it's an experience and some basic inferences can be drawn.

I would also have the students working as qualitative researchers, where "the researcher . . . observes, asks questions, and interacts with research participants" (Glesne and Peshkin 1992, 6). This next step would have my students interviewing people who were entering the building. I've never done this kind of on-campus research before, but here's a preliminary list of activities my students and I might do in preparation (most of the following would be accomplished by my students):

- Request a field trip from our school administration.
- Contact the college administration for permission to conduct the survey.
- Write a letter to the editor of the campus newspaper, copied and sent to the campus police department, explaining the purpose, the date, and times of our work.
- Obtain a bus or, in the case of our school, sometimes solicit *keeper* drivers.
- Write a letter to my substitute teacher to organize my other classes.
- Send a letter of explanation home to the *keepers* of the class involved.
- Run practice interview sessions at school for my students.
- Contact the Dean of Students to see if she or he would speak with us on the subject of gender issues in college.
- Contact faculty or staff of various majors.
- Wear clearly labeled name tags while on campus and have a large sign in front of each building that briefly explains the purpose of our project.
- Take volunteers from the class to staff the various buildings on campus—future science students will probably be more focused if they were outside the science building.
- Work with my student colleagues to develop a series of solid questions to ask the college students and staff members in the front of the building.

Clearly, the amount of work involved is significant. Planning for field trips or any out-of-school adventure is hard work; however, the benefits for our students are clear. In this case, my students would have a chance to spend part of a day on a college campus—many never have had this opportunity. While talking with college students and staff members, the high school students would take the lead as interviewers and learn how to handle a variety of people-to-people situations. The final product of the research experience would have them writing up their own observations while synthesizing the quantitative results and the comments solicited.

Let me emphasize that not all field trip experiences are so complex. But one thing is a given: Whenever I take teenagers beyond the schoolhouse doors, I am thoroughly organized and ready for just about anything.

The Theme of Age: Visiting Elementary Schools and Interviewing Older Folks

As an introduction to the theme of age during second quarter, we watched the 1980s classic movie, *On Golden Pond*, with Katherine Hepburn and Henry Fonda. The story addresses generation differences, parent/child relationships, and communication issues in a thoughtful and an entertaining fashion. Students had an option to write a review or analysis of the movie for their portfolios.

After the movie, each student arranged a daylong visit to an elementary school classroom (early kindergarten to third grade). The purpose? To observe and participate, to teach and learn, to connect and remember and, of course, to escape Room 109. Of all the adventures my kids enjoy, both in and out of the classroom, this is the near-unanimous favorite. In the younger grades, my students feel like kings and queens, and to these little people, they are. By focusing on the elementary school children, my students also discovered more about themselves. Tabitha, a senior, illustrates this in her written reflection of the elementary school experience:

> *Looking back, I think that this visitation helped me in many more ways than just remembering my own elementary experience. I was able to relate to things in my personal life today from a different angle. I remembered that the sun and moon do not hang on my every move and that mistakes are made.*

The whole-world experience of this project begins immediately. Students have to call, write, or meet with an elementary school teacher and set up a time to visit the classroom. For many, this is a harrowing assignment. "Me? Call a teacher? At their home?" Once organized, students must clear their field trips through the school's main office by completing "prearranged absence forms" (see Figure 2–1). This requires that students speak with each of their teachers individually to gain permission to miss class. At that time they will arrange for any makeup work. The form also requires their *keeper's* signature. That's right, a conversation about school between the adult and her or his teen-ager. Finally, the students have to arrange for a ride to and from the elementary school. To an adult, all of this might sound basic. To our students, however, leaving school for a day requires a great deal of thought, planning, and conversation beyond the classroom.

Once I got into the process of affording students out-of-school opportunities, a troublesome public school inequity became fully evident. We all know that top-flight students spend their days in small honors and AP classes taught by veteran teachers who have their acts together. Similarly, special needs students are afforded small classes or, if they have been mainstreamed, often enjoy one-on-one assistance during the school day.

**Mountain Valley High School
Prearranged Absence Request**

Student _____

Reason for Absence _____

Dates student will be absent _____

Period	Course	Teacher Signature/Assignments	Due Date
A			
B			
C			
D			
E			
F			
G			

Teachers: Do you feel this absence is detrimental to this student's academic progress in your class? Add comments below if desired.

A	
B	
C	
D	
E	
F	
G	

Parent/Guardian: I have seen the assignments and comments on this form and given my child permission to be absent. I understand that if the required work is not completed by the deadlines given, my child may not receive full credit for the days missed.

_____
Parent/Guardian Signature

Figure 2–1. MVHS Prearranged Absence Form

Furthermore, it's not uncommon for both groups of students to leave school for one program or another. However, students from the middle and lower academic groupings are rarely afforded these opportunities.

Once I realized this disparity, I worked hard to make sure my middle kids had a similar variety of opportunities. Indeed, these students had difficulty organizing, calling, and daring. But once they got into the experience, in this case an elementary school classroom, many of them blossomed.

The second adventure of the eight-week quarter had my students interviewing a person who was over sixty years old. As with the elementary school visit, this experience took place outside Room 109, and each student had to make all of the arrangements.

In class, we brainstormed a list of thoughts, ideas, and questions that would help stimulate conversation if things got stale. Here are a few samples:

- What is the most important lesson you've ever learned?
- If you could change one thing about your past, what might it be?
- In your eyes, what's the meaning of success?
- What are your favorite books?
- Who were your heroes as a teenager?
- What is your fondest memory?
- Compare teens today with teens of your era.
- What were your goals as a teenager?
- If you have a significant other, how did you meet?
- How have the wars over the years affected your life?
- What about parent rules during your teenage years?
- What responsibilities did you have as a teenager?
- Talk about music, dancing, and social life as a teenager.
- How do you feel morals and values have changed through the years?
- What was your most embarrassing moment?
- Do you have advice for young people today?

We also discussed how some older folks have difficulty with the younger generation.

"My grandfather says kids today are useless," complains Tyler. "I don't want to interview him. I'll get one of his lectures."

"Tyler makes a good point," I interject. "You need to be prepared for everything."

"I just don't want to listen to him anymore, Mr. Kent. It won't be fun," says Tyler. A few of the other kids chime in with similar thinking.

"Here's an idea," I say. "If the person starts a lecture like that, ask them what the older people thought about their generation of teenagers. I bet they'll smile. I also bet it's not much different than today."

A week into the quarter I pass out the following list to help the students stay on track and see the big picture of their quarter's English work:

**109 Portfolio II
Second Quarter: Age**

Here are the basic 109 portfolio requirements for second quarter:

- Forty-eight 150-word journal entries . . . a variety of entries!
- Three to five book projects . . . one of which is written (6 pages plus).
- Five books read . . . a variety of books!
- One highly revised paper (1200-word minimum) over an interview with a person who was a teenager during the 1940s or 1950s.
- One highly revised paper (600-word minimum) over visiting an elementary school classroom, K–3. (Remember to arrange the visit *before* Christmas.)
- One paper that is a revision of a first-quarter paper showing all of the revision work you accomplished.
- OPTIONAL: One paper over *On Golden Pond* if you do not have enough written work in the three papers above. You should have approximately 3000 words in those three papers. Lost? See me.
- Participate by listening and speaking during class.
- SAVE all handouts from Kent.
- A *keeper* letter (parent, guardian, or trusted adult) in response to your portfolio.

Portfolio Due Dates For Each Class:

> 3/4A, English 11—Friday, January 16
> Dead Poets' Class—Tuesday, January 20
> 6/7A, Writing Center—Tuesday, January 20
> 1/2B, English 11—Wednesday, January 21
> 3/4B, Writing Center—Thursday, January 22
> 1/2A, Writing Center—Friday, January 23

Kurt's Experiences with the Age Theme

As I read through Kurt's journal book at the end of the quarter, I noticed a page of scrawled signatures. Kurt's class of first graders wanted to connect with him, and interestingly enough, they chose writing as one of the vehicles.

Just after the kids' signatures, Kurt included the following entry:

> *Well, here I am at Andover School sitting with the first graders. It's story time right now and we are reading* The Polar Express. *I am taking this time to write a journal. The*

kids are really spectacular. I am the coolest thing to them. Everything they want when they get older they ask me about. They ask me if I was still in High School and what grade I was in. What I was doing in their class, and just how old I was. These students are very intuitive and they are so excited. Even as I write this journal the kids are looking at me and wondering what I am doing. The kids are very smart and just looking at them I begin to wonder what they will be when they grow up. It's really weird sitting back and looking at the kids and trying to look into their futures. One student I could see being a super athlete and another a lawyer. One kid was very organized and very bright. Each kid is different and you can almost see them learning. I am grateful to have this experience—I am very glad that I could come here and hang out with the kids. I helped with everything. Already today I have been Mr. Craftsman, gym teacher, playground god, and counting genius. It's a really great experience and I have to go now because story time is over.

This journal entry depicts Kurt's observations and feelings about this experience. What strikes me first is the honesty and energy of his words. These children have treated Kurt as the "coolest thing." What teenager wouldn't want to be idolized this way? What's fascinating to me are his mature teacherlike insights, such as "These students are very intuitive . . ." Further, Kurt's ability to look at these students as future adults (e.g., athletes or lawyers) bodes well for the respect he shows these little people.

Recognizing these youngsters for their "differentness" illustrates Kurt's acceptance of and respect for difference. This openness from a young man his age is extraordinary considering most teenagers' obsessions with the self. At times during this journal entry Kurt disappears; his focus, that of an objective observer, moves exclusively toward the children. Here, we witness a teacher in action.

In Kurt's eight-and-a-half-page essay, "The Skill of Being Young," he recounts the glories of his day with the little people. He also reflects on his own days as a little person at Andover Elementary School:

It was weird going back to the old place. I hadn't been there since I was a student, and the memories came back in waves. I could remember the old soccer matches we used to have at recess under the pine trees, and the swinging long jump competitions. I was amazed at how much I recalled. Inside, the school had changed from what I had remembered. Some of the classrooms were different and everything seemed so much smaller. The "giant" institution that I remembered became more and more just a little building with swings out back.

For those students like Kurt, who returned to the schools they had attended as children, the experience produced a variety of feelings. This connection to their pasts created interesting revelations. It seems clear to me that connecting with the past—making meaning of experiences and seeing how they have affected our days—is key to looking into the future and constructing an image of what we see ourselves becoming.

I am reminded of Bread Loaf teacher James Britton's book, *Prospect and Retrospect* (1982). In the first paragraph of the introduction, written by editor Gordon Pradl, the following words helped shape my understanding of the power of my students' experiences:

> In telling the stories of our reality . . . we assert a future. The future, though apparently beyond our control, is in actuality a continuing alternative, one we actively construct out of our understanding of past events. (1)

As my students begin to realize the connection of the past, present, and future—and often this happens through journal writing—they also begin to see the possibilities of their lives. Certainly, as Pradl professes, "Language powers the future."

For Kurt, leaving my classroom and returning to Andover Elementary School stimulated this reflective writing. The authenticity of his writing is reinforced by the authenticity of place. This is to say that Kurt needed to be there to make this connection complete and his writing genuine.

Kurt's day at school was recorded in the Andover Elementary School's newspaper:

> We had a guest on Tuesday. His name was Kurt Milligan. He is a Mountain Valley student. He came to observe for a research paper he was writing. I believe he was comparing primary education now to long ago. What a great person to have in our room! He was terrific with the children and did a wonderful job working with them. Mrs. K and I thought he'd make an excellent teacher. He was a natural.

The last two lines of the article speak volumes about this young man.

Had this quarter ended with this elementary school experience, Kurt would have been on top of the world. However, in the next phase of the project—interviewing a person who was a teenager in the 1940s or 1950s—he ran into a cantankerous old fellow who wasn't remotely interested in spending time with a teenager. After an abysmal forty-five minutes at the nursing home, Kurt left with little from his interview. This experience left him sad and confused.

Even so, Kurt's reflection at the end of the quarter revealed the significance of the collective experience. He writes, "This class has made me think about certain issues and has made me work out resolutions on my own. I have come to know myself better and what I want to accomplish well after my time here is done."

Throughout his reflection, Kurt makes whole-world connections. He looks at himself as a learner—his strengths and weaknesses—while beginning to see where he would like to be in the future. This is a fascinating look into the life of a young man who is looking forward in the midst of thinking back.

Reading all of my students' reflections and highlighting the meaningful lines proves to be one of the most valuable learning experiences of the school year for me as teacher. I place these quotations in a collection much like the list of excerpts from my students' autobiographies near the beginning of the book. Reading them as a whole helps me make meaning of our experience together.

For more information about this kind of teacher research, see "Writing to Build a Classroom Community" in *Room 109: The Promise of a Portfolio Classroom* (Kent 1997, 21).

Bridges: A Cross-Age Tutoring Project

Over the course of three years, I took full classes of high school students to work in elementary schools with fourth and fifth graders. We went one or two times a week by school bus, and most of my students valued this time a great deal. From editing to co-authoring and producing plays, the teenagers and their "students" learned from one another.

My partner in the elementary schools, Linda Howe, handled the on-site logistics in the younger grades by scheduling class visits with her colleagues. As a bonus, the letters that Linda and I shared back and forth about this pilot program also embraced the craft of teaching in a most meaningful way. Our letter conversations provided the kind of collegiality we teachers dream about.

Bridges created a number of interesting moments, not all of which were positive. The teenagers had an opportunity to observe learning from the teacher's point of view while experiencing the role of teacher, mentor, and older friend. As for the elementary school students, they received one-on-one attention from, in most cases, some pretty neat kids. The younger students also had the opportunity to ask questions about life at the middle and high schools. These conversations, I am sure, assuaged many of their fears about moving to the next level.

The struggles my students encountered throughout the experience helped them learn to cope with and solve a number of problems. And these problems weren't contrived by me in my classroom, i.e., "What changes would you make if you were principal of this school?" These were honest-to-goodness, in-your-face situations.

Ryan stands in front of the class of twenty-two fifth graders. He is their height, but five years older. "OK, who'd like to share their story?"

Not one fifth grader is listening.

"Come on! Pay attention!" Ryan orders.

Still nothing.

He climbs up on the teacher's chair, cups his hands to his lips, and pretends to trumpet an attack. The kids' eyes turn upward and their mouths close.

"So, who wants to read?" asks Ryan, with a smirk of satisfaction amongst the silent smiles.

Julie interviews eleven-year-old Tasha about her life.

"Tell me about your mom," says the perky junior.

Tasha begins to sob. Her mom had died the previous spring from breast cancer.

They sit together quietly.

For a few of the high school students, this was the first time they had been asked to be role models and take charge. They labored with the responsibility. In fact, I remember a tiny fourth grader fiercely eyeing one of my juniors and saying, "Would you stop fooling around? I have to get this work done." The high school kid rolled his eyes and tossed another staple at a girl he was "courting."

Letter from 4th grader to her teacher

4/18

Dear Mrs. C,

I would like to say something about the High School kids. I DON'T LIKE THEM. All they do is talk, talk and talk about there life and thereself. Some of them are o.k. but I don't like Sharon and Jerry. Sometimes Sharon and Jerry don't even help us. They are always fighting and thinking there cool. I don't mind the other kids but some people bug me and get on my nevers.

love,

P.S. If you give this to the High School, can you erase my name. Thanks.

Neither Jerry nor Sharon had ever been leaders. They had no younger siblings and always swam near the bottom of the academic pond. Bridges put them in a position they'd never been in before.

If what Jerry has done effects our visits to the elementary school or puts an end to them, I am going to wreck him.

Michelle, a sophomore
from her daily journal

Helping these teenagers learn how to relate to their protégés required a lot of conversation back in Room 109. There, I would share elementary school journals and letters like the one above. The younger students' words brought about important discussions.

Most of my students realized the Bridges program was a privilege—they loved getting out of school and working with the younger students. Still others found it a hassle. When Sharon and Jerry acted out in Mrs. C's class, the more responsible high school students stepped in, both at the elementary school and back in Room 109. The matter was settled.

For the most part, my students' journals and letters blew me away. Their insights and sensitivities toward the fourth and fifth graders often reflected thinking beyond their years.

You learn more when you're trying to teach
than when you're trying to learn.

> Naomi, a sophomore
> from her Bridges journal

Some days in Bridges proved absolutely dazzling. On one such day, my students put on short plays and readings for Mr. Waite's fifth graders. Eight stations dotted the hallway, the staircase, and the front lawn. Small groups of fifth graders spent eight minutes at each. Jamie dressed in full Native American dress to tell a story he had created; the eleven-year-olds remained captivated. With Kate, Joel, and Janel, the students created an original story in the round using pictures as guides; laughter rolled from the far corner of the hallway. Quiet Matt read a story about a homeless boy; Micaiah sang folk songs; Dana read *Green Eggs and Ham* with real green eggs at his feet. The hour passed quickly and the chattering on the return trip to the high school revealed its success.

Of course, not every class on every day brought about these shining moments. And I did not escape the heat. When my students acted out—fooled around on the playground, chewed gum in class, or violated elementary school expectations—I got the call, or in this case, the letter:

To: Rich Kent
Fr: Crystal
Re: Tutors
My students have been asked to write about their feelings in relation to the high school tutors.

A few of my students have also come to me very upset about some of your students because of comments such as, "It was nice working with you little kids who don't know anything." This has a negative effect on my students' self-esteem. Upon discussing this situation with the principal, I am requesting that the students from your class with negative attitudes not be sent to my class. You will be able to read about specifics in my students' letters.

My first reaction was to boot the high school culprits. Yet in the next moment I realized these students like Sharon and Jerry need this experience most of all. After talking at length with my class, I sent off a letter to Mrs. C requesting a meeting between my high schoolers and her elementary students. The goal was to try and find a solution to the problems. It worked. Mrs. C responded:

> . . . Just sitting watching them talk so freely, I felt a
> lot of excitement. I was very impressed!
> Thanks, Crystal
> P.S. A lot of learning took place today!

Indeed, a lot of learning took place throughout the whole Bridges' experience.

Making Meaning of Bridges: A Practical Exercise

Near the end of my time at the Bread Loaf School of English, my teacher Dixie Goswami introduced an intriguingly simple yet revealing exercise to help us look more closely at our time together. I now use *making meaning* in my classes to help my students see more clearly. This four-step activity gives form and order to what can be chaotic thinking. It may focus on any particular aspect of the class. Among other issues, I have had the students write about Room 109, portfolios, and themselves. In this case we focused on their teaching time in Bridges.

Here's Victoria's *making meaning* about Bridges. I give my students about a minute for each of the first three steps. The last one usually takes five to eight minutes.

Step One: Using single words *name* some of what Bridges is to you:

boring

complicated

new

different

challenging

exchanging

sharing

understanding

annoyed

interesting

unrealistic (at times)

regulations

complain

frustrating

Step Two: Now name the opposite of those terms to create a dialectic. This is important because reconciling opposites or reasoning contrary arguments help us arrive at the truth. ("Huh?") There are always two sides to things. It always comes back to *balance*, the yearlong theme of our class.

boring	exciting
complicated	easy
new	old
different	usual
challenging	ordinary
exchanging	quiet
sharing	keeping
understanding	uncooperative
annoyed	pleasant
interesting	boring
unrealistic (at times)	realistic
regulations	free
complain	?
frustrating	easy

Step Three: Place some of the opposing words in a true sentence about Bridges:

- I like it when kids *share* their ideas and don't *keep* them to themselves.
- It was a very *fun* experience for me when the children were understanding but at times they could be *uncooperative*.
- Staying at the high school all the time gets *boring*, but going to the elementary school is *exciting*.

Step Four: In the final step, we use strict form to help us make meaning. Write one paragraph of five sentences about Bridges using the following guidelines:

Sentence 1   a five-word statement

Sentence 2   a question

Sentence 3   two independent clauses combined by a semicolon

Sentence 4   a sentence with an introductory phrase

Sentence 5   a two-word statement

Teaching is a challenging experience. Could it be any harder? I think it depends on our attitudes; all of us need positive attitudes. Although getting to know these kids was difficult, it eventually got a little easier. We coped.

Here are a few other paragraphs about Bridges that I found particularly interesting:

Teaching has always haunted me. Are teachers as scary as the student thinks they are? I never wanted to teach because I hated teachers; I'm a teacher now. After the experience I hope that the fifth graders think of me as a person, not a teacher. It's helped.
Sydney

I hate teaching fifth graders. Why does Mr. Kent make us teach some of those awful little brats? If I have to go there much longer I will be very upset; I may start yelling at some of the kids. After I yell at them I will be in big trouble and I'll never have to go back. It sucks!!
Sharon

Teaching was an enlightening experience. Did we learn anything from this? We teach them things; they teach us things. Once we got to know them, we became friends. Adventure trek.
Luanne

Making meaning helps my students see the full picture. This activity reveals certain truths about issues or ideas; what's more, such truths may not have been recognized by my students without the formula. From developing a balanced essay to working out life issues, *making meaning* helps my students think more completely.

"How We Teach Writing in M.S.A.D. #43"

Using our school district as a research project gave students in one of my classes a chance to leave the high school and interview teachers throughout the district. Together, my student colleagues and I came up with a series of questions on teaching writing. Our end product would be the story of writing and writing instruction throughout the district. The piece would be in the form of a synthesis of quotations connected with a narrative. I would author the final product.

The responsibility for contacting the teachers to be interviewed remained with the twenty-six students involved. They also arranged for their own dismissal from school, normally during our class or a study hall, and for transportation to the district schools. These obligations added to the students' experience. We divided the district's master list of teachers by student preference. The most popular teachers were ultimately assigned by a furious game of "rock, paper, scissors." (We should all be so admired.)

Before the students headed off, I sent a letter of explanation to each school's secretary. I asked for this notice to be displayed prominently in the staff room, posted in the staff bathrooms next to the mirrors, and placed in the staff notices.

My students' interview notes and final narratives served as two of their formal papers for their quarter-end portfolios.

Here are the questions we asked the district teaching staff:

1. Describe your personal writing process.
2. Are you a regular writer? Do you share your writing with your students (e.g., journal, diary, frequent letters, professional work, work assigned to students, fiction, or poetry)?
3. Give an example of the writing process you encourage your students to follow.
4. Describe or provide examples of various writing assignments.
5. Do your students write across the curriculum (e.g., science and math)? Do your students use learning logs?
6. How often do your students write?
7. How do you utilize computers or word processors in your writing curriculum? How often?
8. Approximate the percentage of assignments you require from your students in each of the following types of written discourse[1] (please know that we realize that these kinds of writing overlap):

Transactional: this type of writing aims to inform, persuade, or instruct an audience in clear, conventional, concise prose. Examples are term papers, science and history reports, essay examinations, and book reviews.

Expressive: this type of writing is self-expressive and reveals the speaker and her/his consciousness. Examples of this include diaries, journals, personal letters—this type of writing is characterized by first-person pronouns, informal style, and colloquial diction.

Poetic: this type of writing is also called creative writing. It is language which functions as art. Examples include fiction, poetry, drama, and song.

[1](Adapted from the work of Nancy Martin's *Mostly About Writing* [1983] and James Britton's *Prospect and Retrospect* [1982].)

During the summer, I narrowed the final product of the inquiry to six pages. I mailed the final copy to my student colleagues for any comments or corrections. That fall, we distributed the story of how we teach writing in S.A.D. #43.

Portfolio Projects Outside of School

In response to class themes or books read, students produce three to five projects per nine-week quarter. At the heart of these book projects is an understanding of Howard Gardner's work with multiple intelligences (1983) and Thomas Armstrong's inner genius (1998). These creations celebrate my students' talents and add to their growth in many ways, the most important of which may be dealing with people beyond the classroom.

After reading the book *Pretty Girls in Little Boxes: The Making and Breaking of Elite Gymnasts and Figure Skaters* (1996) by Joan Ryan, Tanya produced a video explaining the different events of gymnastics. This took a good deal of organization on her part. She interviewed gymnasts, coaches, judges, and parents at the community center; she arranged for different athletes to demonstrate different events for the video; and she worked with an editor at the local public access channel who helped produce the final video. For seventeen-year-old Tanya, the experience of calling the editor at the public access channel was a first. In her journal she wrote, "Before this I'd never called someone I didn't know and asked for help. I was very nervous and wrote down notes like you said so when I got on the phone I wouldn't sound dumb."

Kevin studied Robert Frost through the quarter. By the end of his study, he decided it was time to take a pilgrimage to Frost's cabin on the grounds of Middlebury College's Bread Loaf School of English. The journey is an eight-hour round trip. Similarly, as I mentioned at the beginning of the book, Darcy and Dusty traveled via mountain bikes to the riverside home of the late Maine author Louise Dickinson Rich after reading her autobiography, *We Took to the Woods*.

The centerpiece of my young adult novel, *The Mosquito Test*, is the initiation for The Tribe. Prospective members are boys aged nine to eleven. For the test the kids strip down to their underwear and sit on a log during Maine's "bug months" of April, May, and June. To pass the test the boy could not slap, itch, or move for ten minutes while the mosquitoes and black flies feasted.

This challenge seemed just the thing for two of my students, Dave and Jack. So in celebration of *The Mosquito Test* the two sophomores trucked out into the deep woods on their four-wheelers. They setup the video, stripped down to their boxer shorts, and sat still for ten solid minutes. In class we roared watching the video of the two boys squirming as the bugs did the deed.

Emily hikes to the top of Angel's Falls and paints a watercolor after reading *Nature I Loved* by Bill Geagan. With his grandfather, Ryan builds a coffin celebrating Edgar Allan Poe. John spends an hour interviewing an executive with a large supermarket firm after reading a series of business magazines; Lori attends a lecture on the Holocaust at Bates College after reading Art Spiegelman's *Maus I* and *Maus II*. In response to these experiences, some of my students write summaries for their journals, others send off letters to the folks they visited. A number carry the project to another level by writing a paper on the experience. Most of the time, the choice is theirs.

One Book Project: A Weekend in the Woods

"As a boy growing into a man in a world of everlasting chaos, there is constant pressure to be successful. I have long wanted to ignore this pressure and spend time alone with my thoughts. I do not get this chance often because of the number of people living in my household and the amount of noise they create."

So begins Jeffrey's essay, "Weekend in the Woods." In response to Thoreau's *Walden* and Geagan's *Nature I Loved*, Jeffrey took the weekend off from work at a local hardware store. "After reading these two books, I knew that being alone in the woods would affect me. The main reason why I knew this was because I have never been alone before and I could see how both Henry David Thoreau and Bill Geagan were truly changed by their time in solitude."

Jeff, who captained our championship soccer team, settled into a one-room cabin on the quiet shores of Lake Webb here in the western mountains of Maine. He set off on this late October journey to seek more of himself. During his stay, he wrote twenty-two handwritten pages of journal entries as he struggled with the alone time and with what he perceived as the wilderness. Here's a small collection of lines from his writings:

What the hell am I going to do with myself up here?

The forest makes a lot of noise when you're alone.

Hopefully before I leave I will be able to walk through the woods without worrying what's behind me.

There is an emptiness inside me right now. I can't figure out if it is because I haven't seen a single person in over eight hours or if I just miss Rumford and everyone there.

I want to give someone a call, but I don't want to sound like a wimp because I am getting homesick.

One tends to appreciate things more when alone.

For some reason the morning feels like a new life.

You have to be alone more often to appreciate the benefits of it.

When I got home this afternoon I didn't want to deal with anyone. I tried to write, like I did at the cabin, but people kept making noise and the silence I was used to was not there and I got pretty upset. I was happy to see people but I wasn't happy to listen to all of their shit.

Jeff's weekend adventure was, at best, unsettling. "It seemed strange not to have someone to discuss my thoughts and feelings with . . . At times I was even talking to myself out loud so I would not forget what my voice sounded like."

The experience of facing ourselves is invaluable. For young people readying themselves for independent study—or for life after school—the simple act of being alone for a period of time can add to their foundation of self-knowledge. Outward Bound realizes this when they ship their charges out on *solos* with a book of readings and scant rations. Like many, Jeff couldn't see the good of his alone time while he was in the midst of the experience. As he came to realize, not all important experiences are fun, exciting, or something to write home about.

Two years after his weekend in the woods, now a sophomore at the University of Vermont, Jeff looks back at his time alone with a philosophical perspective. "In some ways that experience prepared me for college—for being alone at college. I know it matured my thinking. I think I grew up a lot during that weekend—I learned about myself."

Afterthought

After writing this small section about Jeff's experience, I've decided to make "time alone" part of my yearlong curriculum for all students. I'll begin this coming year by offering it as an extra credit option. Once I see how the kids take hold of the opportunity, I'll be better equipped to determine if I can require the experience.

As always, my students become my most effective teachers.

D.A.R.E. Role Models, Peer Helpers, AWAP, Community Service Projects...

Programs such as D.A.R.E. Role Models, Peer Helpers, and the Abused Women's Advocacy Program (AWAP) provide opportunities for my students to talk and perform outside of the classroom to a wide variety of audiences. Our school encourages but as yet does not mandate community service projects for students. Even so, students' community service projects are noted on their transcripts as a Pass/Fail assessment, and they become part of their district portfolio, a collection of "best works" kept from kindergarten through twelfth grade. Students who perform community service are excused from school during their projects.

With encouragement from me, students involved in these organizations use one of their speeches or a presentation in lieu of an English assignment. Further, sometimes our class serves as a practice audience for these young volunteers. This is as authentic as it gets.

Enriching the Classroom with Multiple Intelligences

When Teatra dances, our hearts quicken. With his guitar and a sweet tenor's voice, Mark helps us settle into the moment. When he sings "Fire and Rain," we join in. Katie's conversation skills bring out the best in each of us while Tia's cartoons delight. Amanda writes provocative poems; Kristin whispers to calm our latest visitor, her prize-winning lamb; Aaron figures out computer problems with ease; and Georgianna's journals claw deep within her soul to a place of meaning.

When shared in our English class, my students' gifts help us see a piece of literature or an idea in a unique light. Helping my students try out and develop a variety of intelligences is an important part of my job and an important precursor to ISP. The most effective classrooms and teachers, projects and assignments, embrace learning differences. It's true, in terms of teaching and learning we have moved away from "How smart are you?" to "How are you smart?" The result? Our students create and deliver meaning and Room 109 becomes a place of experimentation and daring.

"I don't do painting," proclaims Jeff, a hulking linebacker on our 7-1 football team.

"I bet you do," I say.

A few weeks later Jeff's project, a charcoal abstract of Mark Twain, is ready.

In my students' portfolio work and in their year-end ISP, I require products that touch on Howard Gardner's Multiple Intelligences (1983, 1993). Expanding my students' intelligences helps build more complete people who are more willing and able to accept all of life's offerings.

Reviewing Dr. Gardner's intelligences frequently helps my students and me think of new and exciting ways to portray books and ideas. If Room 109 is to be a place of abundant learning, all of these intelligences need to be nurtured.

Logical-Mathematical—this intelligence focuses on reasoning. Logical-mathematical students show strengths in organizing, questioning, calculating, and experimenting; they're good at solving puzzles and learning facts. The classes that normally embrace this intelligence are history, math, and science. An example of this intelligence used in a Room 109 project would be Jeremy's *Trail 109*, a hiking trail designed through the Longfellow Mountains here in western Maine.

Spatial-Visual—this intelligence focuses on pictures and images. Spatial-visual students are the artsy kids who show talent in illustrating, drawing, sketching; they love graphics or producing videos. The classes that normally embody these intelligences are geometry, art, and CAD (computer aided drafting). An example of this intelligence used in a Room 109 project would be from Susan's Alzheimer's study. She painted a brooding surrealistic piece that depicted the family's narrowing view of the patient's personality.

Naturalist—this intelligence, the most recent, focuses on the natural world. Naturalist students are connected to the outdoors and enjoy astronomy, meteorology, long walks in the woods, and exploring. Most of these students love animals. Classes that normally focus on a naturalist theme include science classes and outdoor education classes. An example of this intelligence in a Room 109 project would be Dawn and Adam's nature studies or the course Darcy took at the Hurricane Island Outward Bound program.

Linguistic-Verbal—this intelligence focuses on the use of words. Linguistic-verbal students celebrate language through writing, reading, speaking, and interpreting. Many classes deal with language arts skills and activities. An example of this intelligence in a Room 109 project would be Donna's teaching Spanish to first and second graders during her ISP.

Interpersonal—this intelligence focuses on communicating with other people. These students have people skills. Any class that encourages group projects or cooperative learning activities nourishes a student's interpersonal intelligence. An example of this intelligence in a Room 109 project would be Peter's internship in a public relations office at a nearby ski area.

Musical-Rhythmic—this intelligence focuses on melodies and rhythms. My musical–rhythmic students love to sing and play instruments. Classes such as band, music theory, and chorus focus on this intelligence. An example of a musical–rhythmic project would be Jason's ISP of drumming throughout the world.

Intrapersonal—this intelligence focuses on reflective thinking. Those students who prosper within this intelligence are in touch with their own feelings. They enjoy self-assessing and quiet moments reflection; they usually love to journal. Most classes, at least through the assigning of homework, nurture the student's intrapersonal intelligence. A 109 project that typifies the student's reflective skills is Jeff's weekend alone in the woods.

Bodily-Kinesthetic—this intelligence focuses on bodily movements. Students who dance, like role-playing, or love to run and play games are those who feel comfortable within this intelligence. Obviously, physical education, dance, and sports focus on this intelligence. One example of a project from Room 109 is Adam's research study of plyometrics, a series of muscle-strengthening exercises. An added benefit: this project helped his high jumping and basketball abilities.

Over the years my classroom has evolved to reflect my students' many talents. Some days Room 109 resembles an artist's studio; other days a writer's den. Once the room was transformed into a Buddhist temple, and not too long ago it was a 1970s discotheque. (I am still shuddering from that bell-bottomed, opened-shirt retromoment.)

I like to think of this little 20-by 26-foot room as a place of possibility. During ISP, it is.

3

ISP: The First Week

My Dear Students,

As third quarter fades from our memories, it's time to begin independent study projects. You have the next week to think, plan, and organize. Let's review the possibilities of ISP.

109 independent study is a chance to select a focus for your own English studies. You may work by yourself or with one other person. These studies have run the full spectrum, as you have seen by a few of the speakers we've heard over the past couple of months. You have also seen that these projects are both a lot of fun *and* a lot of work.

All ISP must have certain English class guidelines as part of the process and the final product. What does this mean? Think about Room 109: different students, different interests, different focuses, different portfolios. In terms of English/language arts, students here are always reading, writing, listening, speaking, viewing, observing, presenting, and performing. Additionally, as we have discovered, you may very well end up videoing, interviewing, photographing, apprenticing, building, painting or cooking. So, your independent study project needs to reflect this kind of English work, even if your focus is being a game warden or a microbiologist.

Let's talk about some of the possibilities. Last year, one young woman worked at Meroby Elementary School with a third-grade teacher. She tutored kids; read and studied college books on teaching and learning; kept a journal of her work; observed other elementary school classrooms and wrote her observations; composed essays about teaching in the elementary school; wrote an essay about learning environments (where people learn best); videotaped a class and showed it to her 109 colleagues; visited the University of Maine at Farmington to interview an education professor to learn more about teacher education; and interviewed me about teaching.

51

Her final portfolio reflected an in-depth study on teaching and learning at the elementary school level. This year, she's studying at a university to become a teacher. Now, don't worry. Just because you study microbiology for ISP doesn't mean you have to head off to college for this. The purpose is to look at different occupations or enjoy an in-depth investigation while managing your time and producing quality work.

Five students last year studied poets. They read the poet's biography (or autobiography); read a number of books of poetry by the writer; and wrote a series of papers, poems, and journals. For projects, some painted pictures, others built "things" to celebrate the author. Others, when possible, traveled to the poet's home or visited the college library where the poet's work is collected. When it comes to English work, everything balances out.

Often, I hear students joking about studying four-wheelers or mall shopping for an English independent study project. Either can be done, believe it or not. As long as your plan includes elements of our language arts class (e.g., reading, writing . . .) your ISP will be approved. Take a close look at the various Final Product forms from last year when I pass them around today. These will help you plan your own ISP.

Some of you are pretty excited about the prospect of escaping school and English class (thanks a lot). Of course, this can be done. In fact, I encourage it. Get out of here! But remember: You need *keeper* permission, a prearranged absence form from the office, and my approval. If you have a study hall before or after English, you can escape for three hours during school. Remember, though, you must have a plan and a contact out of school. And when you say you're going to a certain place . . . you know the rest.

Next week you will present your ISP idea to your classmates. You may use the April Prospectus as a guide. Try to keep your talk to a minimum— only a couple of minutes. We'll add any suggestions (e.g., contacts, books, Web sites) after you have presented.

That's enough for now. I look forward to chatting with you about your ISP plans. Have fun and think large.

YLET,
Rich Kent

Organizing

All through the school year I have talked about independent study projects in class and with individual students so when fourth quarter comes around I am not springing a new idea on them. Some of my students are already focused and ready to go once third quarter ends. Some knew the previous summer how they would spend their final quarter. Still others are deciding among a few different ISP ideas. I begin the quarter with a class letter like the one above. I use letters because the students can continually refer to them.

Keeping *keepers* informed

I require *keeper* permission for ISP. In my first letter home in September, I mention the fourth-quarter projects. Then, right at the end of third quarter, I write a more in-depth letter about ISP. Needless to say, informing the adults in my students' lives from the outset keeps problems ("You're going to go fishing for nine weeks for English class?") to a minimum. As I mentioned earlier on, *keepers* also have to sign our school's prearranged absence forms before their student goes anywhere.

Fourth Quarter
Room 109

Dear Moms and Uncles, Dads and Grandmas, Aunts and Friends . . .
Keepers of 109,

It's time for independent study projects (ISP) here in Room 109. I wanted to touch base and give you a bit more information about your child's final quarter of English work.

ISP is an opportunity for our students to experience choice, decision making, and out-of-school opportunity while looking into a career or exploring an interest. Some people call this experience "school to work"; I call it "school to life." The project is based in English/language arts. This means that students will be doing a good deal of reading, writing, listening, speaking, viewing, observing, presenting, and performing. In fact, the final product is the not-so-dreaded-anymore P-Word: portfolio. Students also present various projects similar to those from the first three quarters.

In the past, ISP students have job-shadowed doctors and lawyers, loggers and store managers, teachers and pilots. They have investigated circa 1940 abandoned cars, participated in archaeological digs of 19th century farms, fished the lakes and streams of western Maine, and studied the geology of Mount Washington. In short, they've done a bit of everything.

Attached to this letter is a sample ISP prospectus. This plan gives you an idea of what's necessary for preliminary approval. Once your student brings her or his prospectus home, please go over it with the student. If you agree with the work, sign it. If you have any concerns at all, please call me or drop by. You must be confident with this project.

During the course of the last quarter, you will be faced with the decision of whether you want your student to leave school for this experience. Your permission is a must. If the student will leave school for part of the ISP, expect to see a prearranged absence form for you to sign.

Independent study projects are both a good deal of work and a good deal of fun. With your support and mine, these young people can truly have a brilliant learning experience. Thank you for your cooperation.

Warmly,

Rich Kent

Presentations by former ISP Students

Having former students come in to talk about their ISP makes sense. Their talks add a certain reality to the planning of the projects. It's one thing to hear your teacher say you've got to stay organized and stay caught up, but when a person about your age is sounding the alarm, the words resonate a bit more truth.

This year, for the first time, I scheduled model ISP presentations beginning the week after winter break. I want all of my students to begin early the process of thinking about and selecting a topic; I want them to play with ideas and seek out possibilities. Three or four, 10-minute presentations staggered throughout January, February, and March proves just enough to whet my students' imaginations.

Often, my classes include students who have taken my course before. These 109ers earn extra credit by speaking to their fellow classmates about their previous year's ISP experience. They bring in their projects and ISP portfolios to share.

One mistake I made earlier on was bringing in students who were exceptional ISP students and whose projects were of professional quality. I thought this would be motivational, but these superb independent study projects actually discouraged a number of my middle- and lower-level students. It would be like me going to a basketball camp and having the six-foot-six instructor slam dunk the ball, saying, "You, too, will be slamming the ball home in just a few short weeks." *It ain't gonna happen.* Now, I work to bring in a variety of ISP presenters that represent a balanced spectrum.

Themes from the previous year

Looking at the breadth of previous independent study projects illustrates the depth of interests my students enjoy. Sharing these themes with my present students excites them and helps these young adults play with their own ideas.

Skim through this year's list in Figure 3–1 and see if you don't get excited. Think about the diversity, the possibility, and the discovery happening in and around a public school classroom.

Model ISP forms

Another way to help students see the potential of independent study projects is to share one set of model ISP forms (e.g., April Prospectus, May

Nature studies

The life of an architect

Books and their movies

Developing a multimedia CD

Training and caring for animals

Picasso

Drawing on the right side of the brain

Snowboarding

British literature

Reading and writing short stories

Teenagers and religion

Opera

Sports writing

Weight lifting and fitness training

Travel

The poet Wallace Stevens

Running

Black and white photography

Utah

Impressionism and Van Gogh

Child development

medicine

Modern dance

Gender issues

Working with Alzheimer's patients

Reading and writing poetry

Sports medicine

Music appreciation

Native American Indians

Reading Stephen King

Belgium

Zen and the art of mountain biking

Music and me

New England authors

Kenneth Roberts

Magic

Growing up diabetic

The Beatles

Nature photography

Basketball

The 20th Maine

High jumping (track event)

The attack at Pearl Harbor

Art and selected artists

Angels

Children's behavior

Fishing and boat building

Living a writer's life

Motorcycling

Multicultural literature

Buddhism

Hiking in Maine

Student teaching

Mark Twain

Mount Washington

Internships in the business world

Rock walls

Sports psychology

Police work

A close look at a car accident

Working as a golf professional

The law

Dance: classical ballet

Serial killers

Life as a day care director

Camping and hiking

California

Relationships

The life of a radio tech

Role playing and D&D

Boat building

1980s entertainment

Coast Guard

Allopathic medicine

Environmental studies

Men and women in conversation

Religious studies

The music of our lives

Inequality

Reading *War and Peace*

Gay, lesbian, and bisexual studies

Sylvia Plath and Ted Hughes

Osteopathic medicine

Learning and schooling

Boston Marathon

Motocross

Learning styles

Being a secretary

Healthy living

Emerging through reading

On Garland Pond

Mind, body, and spiritual healing

Benedict Arnold's Trail

Plants

Elementary education

Rap music

Flying

Figure 3–1. One Year of Independent Study Themes

1st Check-up, Final Product). I also pass around copies of Final Product forms from the year before. It helps if my present students can connect with former students—it's the old "If-she-can-do-it-so-can-I" syndrome. Looking through other students' thinking and planning creates an ideal.

In Figures 3–2 to 3–4, I am including a complete set of ISP forms.

At-a-Glance ISP outlines

I have a number of At-a-Glance ISP outlines available for students to use as topic suggestions and to a stimulate their thinking as they expand their own study. It's fairly easy to develop these outlines. I asked my friend and bird lover Monica Wood to make suggestions for the one in Figure 3–5 on birding. For other At-a-Glance outlines see the appendix.

Teacher Organization

Over the years I have gotten better and better at facilitating ISP. Years of managing kids and their projects have made me this way. Some might say this is a trial by fire; I like to think of it as on-the-job training. As with classroom teaching, supervising independent study projects is a craft.

To help my students create rich, meaningful experiences, I must make certain that my own notes and record keeping stay organized. The following are simple discoveries I have made:

The paperwork

From the teacher's side, staying organized does not have to be a task. I must admit that I am a bit persnickety about staying coordinated. I place all the ISP forms into separate three-ring binders according to class period. Each of the three forms—the April Prospectus, the May Check-up, and the Final Product—has its own color. Whenever I use color-coded paper, I select lighter shades for ease of photocopying. With separate binders and distinct paper color, the chance of misplacing a student's ISP forms is minimal.

Next, each student's form is placed alphabetically in the binder; then, I number each form in the upper right-hand corner. At the front of each binder, I place a numbered class list. This simple system keeps my ISP life fairly organized.

Our school has one of those automatic-feed copiers. With that, I can copy all the forms in a matter of minutes, so students have duplicates.

Staying in touch

During fourth quarter, I formally interview students when I first approve their April Prospectus. I formally interview them again at the three- and seven-week marks. I informally interview my students a great deal. We chat continually about their discoveries or travels, their hangups or sources.

Room 109 Independent Study
April Prospectus

Name   Aaron Gagnon   **Class Period**   Silver D

Phone   555-9051   **Grade in School**   Junior

Title of Project   Mount Washington and its history

Partner(s)   E. J. Martin

Two- to three-sentence description   We are going to research Mt. Washington—the Cog Railway, weather, hiking, and skiing Tuckerman's Ravine.

Proposed Reading: **1.** *The Story of Mount Washington*
                            2. *Into Thin Air*
                            3. Cog R.R. brochure
                            4. MW's Web Site
                            5.

Proposed Writing: **1.** Journals, 30?
                            2. Narrative paper on skiing Tuck's, formal
                            3. History of Cog, formal
                            4.
                            5.

How will you spend your in-class time?   Reading books on Mount Washington and related subjects. Getting info on Internet. Maybe go and interview some people. Watch MW historical movie by W. Holden.

Out-of-School Activities: Skiing Tuckerman's, maybe riding Cog Railway and driving up the Auto Road, hike Mount Washington, go to the Weather Observatory Museum.

Presentation at the End of Project: Not sure yet. Maybe a slide show?

What will be in your final Independent Study portfolio?   Pictures of the mountain and related things. Papers. Journals. Poetry.

APPROVED BY:

/s/ Richard Kent, Teacher of English
/s/ Rosemary E. Gagnon
Keeper (Parent, Guardian, trusted adult)

Figure 3–2. April Prospectus

Room 109 Independent Study
May 1st

Three-Week Check-Up

Name   Aaron Gagnon   **Class Period**   Silver D

Phone   555-9051   **Grade in School**   Junior

Title of Project   Mount Washington and its history

Partner(s)   E. J. Martin

Two- to three-sentence description   We are going to research Mt. Washington—the Cog Railway, weather, hiking, and skiing Tuckerman's Ravine.

What Reading Have You Accomplished:
I am in the middle of *The Story of Mount Washington*. We have read a whole bunch about the mountain on the Internet—I have placed the articles in my portfolio. Read the pamphlets and brochures about the Cog Railway.

What Writing Have You Accomplished:
Started a paper on our Tuck's experience. 12 Journals.

Rate your use of in-class time:

Very Strong   ⟨**Strong**   **Good**⟩   **OK**   **Weak**

Out-of-School Activities Accomplished (e.g., Interviews, Travel):
Skied Tuck's, took pictures, went for a ride around the mountain, watched Dr. Holden's film, talked to you.

What does your Presentation at the End of the Quarter look like Now:
Not sure yet. Probably a talk, a reading, visual stuff.

General Comments on Your Performance so far: I am going to get an A.

Figure 3–3. Three-Week Check-Up

Room 109 Independent Study
Final Product

Name   Aaron Gagnon   **Class Period**   Silver D

Phone   555-9051   **Grade in School**   Junior

Title of Project   Mount Washington and its history

Partner(s)   E. J. Martin

Two- to three-sentence description   Our project is over Mount Washington—the Cog Railway, weather, hiking, and skiing Tuckerman's Ravine.
Reading accomplished (e.g., books, articles):
1. *The Story of Mount Washington* by F. Allen Burt
2. *Railway to the Stars: The Cog Railway*
3. Twenty Internet articles—in portfolio
4. *Into Thin Air*

Writing accomplished:
1. "End over End" The story about our trip to Tuck's
2. "Road to Heaven" The history of Mount Washington
3. "History of the Cog"
4. Short story about hiking Mount Washington
5. 25 Journals

In-school activities: Writing journals, reading, Internet searches, editing papers, planning.

Out-of-school activities: Reading books, writing, skiing Tuckerman's, hiking, driving around the mountain taking pictures.

Final Presentation of Project will include: Pictures, video, and a brief talk. We made a slide board that the workers used on the Cog Railway.

Anything more in your Independent Study portfolio?   Pictures of the mountain and various sights.

Assess your performance:

Below Average/Average/Honors/High Honors

I have put a lot of work into this study since the quarter started. I want an A.

Figure 3–4. ISP Final Product Form

Title: Birding

Description: The study of birding, from a field-experience perspective.

Suggested Reading:
A Field Guide to the Birds, Roger Tory Peterson (best for beginners)
The Audubon Society Encyclopedia of Birds, John K. Terres (research)
How to Attract, House, and Feed Birds, Walter Schutz (projects)

Suggested Writings:
A field-notes journal that records time, place, and nature of bird sightings; field marks to unfamiliar birds; other observations.
Personal essay on the meditative quality of birding
An informative paper on how to recognize common yard birds such as cardinal, house sparrow, house finch, oriole, etc.

Audio-visual resources:
Birds of North America, Thayer's Birding Software (CD-ROM)

Web site:
www.birding.com

Out-of-school activities:
Accompany an experienced birder on a bird walk
Set up a feeder and monitor traffic
Join a field trip sponsored by Audubon or other organizations

In-school activities:
Set up a feeder outside the classroom window
Bring in a display of common birds and quiz the class

Presentation:
Slide presentation of familiar birds
Slide presentation of one family of birds, pointing out differences in field marks (e.g., sparrows, finches)
A demonstration of bird calls
A demonstration of how to build a feeder or birdhouse

Figure 3–5. At-a-Glance ISP Outlines

When I interview students about their ISP, I make notes on the April Prospectus and the May Check-up sheet. I date each entry. A quick glance at these forms keeps me connected to each student's progress. One thing I've noticed about myself as an ISP consultant, I write a lot more notes on students' forms now than when I first began. I guess it's the teacher-researcher in me. Plus, I think it shows the students that I am totally involved in what they're doing.

During workshop time, when students are busy, I find myself paging through the ISP forms. Sometimes I'll come up with an idea for a student's project and place a sticky note on the form so that it shows outside the class binder. When that class and that particular student arrive, I pass on my suggestion.

If the student has an ISP that keeps her out of class, I may send my suggestion to the student's homeroom or to her particular work site. In some cases I may also dash off an E-mail.

Accountability

Since both 109 ISP plans and prearranged absence forms from the school are signed by the *keepers*, I am in a pretty good position when it comes to accountability. If a student says, "I'm going to be at Ms. Maureen's Nursery School on Thursday," and the student decides to head off to the mall instead, that kid has lied to the school, the teacher, and the folks on the home front. Knowing this keeps most kids on the ISP straight and narrow.

Fortunately, I am not in the position of having to check up on the students' whereabouts when they have signed out of school for the day. It would be impossible for me to do that with all the students who head out the front door. In chatting with former students about ISP, they tell me they went where they were supposed to go and did what they were supposed to do. Some stretched lunch hours or stopped at stores on the way back from an experience, but I haven't found anyone yet who simply blew off an entire task. (Don't think I am naive enough not to know that someone out of 900-plus ISP students over the years hasn't skipped out on a responsibility!)

Saying "thank you"

The ISP forms help me recognize those people in and out of school who have helped my students with their projects. I try to drop a postcard to each person who has served as an ISP mentor. One good life lesson is that I make sure my students write thank-you notes to all those who have contributed to their projects.

Five Basic ISP Themes

It seems somewhat helpful to look at independent study projects as fitting under certain general headings. The following are the five basic ISP themes with examples of each. Notice that some of the studies would certainly fit under more than one heading.

Academic/Research

research a writer and her work

study opera

research weight lifting

study classical ballet

Hobby/Life Passion

study snowboarding

research marathon training

study fly tying

research the history of motorcycles

Career

working as a police office

on being a teacher

the life of an architect

living the life of a lawyer

Multithemed

Zen and the art of mountain biking

art, nature, and hiking

French cooking and French culture

modern dance, gender issues

Independent Reading

War and Peace

The poetry and life of Wallace Stevens

multicultural literature

American literature

WRITTEN PROJECTS

advertisement
autobiography
biography
booklet
book report
characterization
checklist
classification
commercial
comic strip
compare and contrast
credo
crossword puzzle
description
diary
dictionary
editorial
field manual
guidebook
handbook
handouts
joke book
journal
letter
list
magazine
manual
myth
newspaper
newspaper headlines
notebook
observation
outline
pamphlet
picture dictionary
play
poem
questions
report
story
story problems
synthesis
test
word search
worksheet

VERBAL PROJECTS

book report
book on tape
characterization
commercial
compare and contrast
description
dialogue
interview
jingle
joke
monologue
musical
myth
rap
recording
sales talk
song
speech
story

KINESTHETIC PROJECTS

apparatus
archeological dig
charade
dance
demonstration
dramatization
experiment
field trip
finger puppets
game
invention
mime
musical
papier maché
puppets
recipe
role play
signing

VISUAL PROJECTS

banner
blueprint
book cover
bookmark
bulletin board
calendar
cartoon
chart
collage
design
diorama
display
drawing
equipment
flannel board
flower arrangement
game
graph
invention
map mobile
model
mosaic
mural
painting
pattern
photograph
picture
picture dictionary
poster
puzzle
scrapbook
sculpture
sign
slide show
tapestry
terrarium
time line
video
wanted poster
weaving
woodworking

Figure 3–6. Suggested Products for ISP Presentations

Suggested Products for ISP

In Figure 3–6 I have included a small listing of possible products for ISP. I ask students to have a rich variety for their regular quarter work as well as for their independent study projects.

Student Presentations and Postings

Students have one week to select their ISP topic(s). After this period, they stand and present their ideas to class. After the presentation, usually four or five students make suggestions for books, personal contacts, or projects. This sharing is one way to maintain our classroom community.

Students also post their ISP theme on our Room 109 site. By doing this, students from all of my classes can connect. I encourage students to E-mail suggestions to one another; I award extra credit to those who do so.

An Aside: Distinguishing Treasure from Trash: Information Literacy

Much of what my students do during independent study projects requires the ability to access, evaluate, and use information from multiple formats (e.g., newspapers, magazines, books, videos, CD-ROMs, and the Web). They work toward becoming information literate.

Today, students are flooded with information options. It's my job to empower learners to make effective use of that information. Fortunately, state and district programs are striving in earnest to help teachers grow as information specialists. For those of us who grew up in the days of "the encyclopedia as primary source," learning the ins and outs of information literacy is a challenge.

The American Library Association and Association for Educational Communications and Technology (1998) have developed information literacy standards for student learning in their publication *Information Power: Building Partnerships for Learning.* Looking at these standards in a collection helped me recognize the various minilessons and talks I had to deliver during the course of the school year. Here is a section from Chapter 2, "Information Literacy Standards for Student Learning." I print out these standards and discuss each with my students, asking them to offer up examples of each standard.

Information Literacy

Standard 1: The student who is information literate accesses information efficiently and effectively.

Standard 2: The student who is information literate evaluates information critically and competently.

Standard 3: The student who is information literate uses information accurately and creatively.

Independent Learning

Standard 4: The student who is an independent learner is information literate and pursues information related to personal interests.

Standard 5: The student who is an independent learner is information literate and appreciates literature and other creative expressions of information.

Standard 6: The student who is an independent learner is information literate and strives for excellence in information seeking and knowledge generation.

Social Responsibility

Standard 7: The student who contributes positively to the learning community and society is information literate and recognizes the importance of information to a democratic society.

Standard 8: The student who contributes positively to the learning community and to society is information literate and practices ethical behavior in regard to information and information technology.

Standard 9: The student who contributes positively to the learning community and to society is information literate and participates effectively in groups to pursue and generate information

Independent study projects help turn students into information seekers. "How do I get the depth charts for Richardson Lake?" "I can't find the address to the dream research institute in Portland." "Who's the head of public relations for L. L. Bean?"

As with life's journey, the questions never end.

4

The Academic/Research ISP

Renae's Project: A Study of Sylvia Plath and Ted Hughes

When Tom Newkirk of the University of New Hampshire English faculty sat down to speak with Renae, I knew he would ask plenty of probing questions in a kind and inviting way. I also knew that Renae would handle whatever Tom mustered up.

I tried to eavesdrop from my desk across the room, but all I could hear were bits and pieces. But what I observed were two thinkers—two scholars—sharing ideas and making discoveries. At one point I heard Tom say, "I'd never thought of that." I knew all along that Renae had done her ISP homework—now I knew she had done it well.

Offering Renae the opportunity to follow her passionate interest in Sylvia Plath gave this high school student and young poet an opportunity to grow as a researcher, scholar, and thinker. ISP can do just that. These projects don't always turn my students into experts, but they do open important doors.

I have included Renae's Final Product form (see Figure 4–1). Notice how much work Renae accomplished on her own. As an English teacher I couldn't imagine assigning this much work to a senior student during the last quarter of the year.

When Renae presented her final project in class, I could feel the power she had gained through her study. Watching a confident high school student strut her academic stuff for thirty minutes has to be one of the most rewarding aspects of independent study projects.

During her talk and reading of Plath's work, Renae explained the "white glove" procedure for inspecting Plath's original manuscripts during her visit to Smith College. All of us laughed when she admitted, "I just had to slip off a glove and touch the real thing."

Plath's poetry influenced Renae's own writing. Here's one of my favorites:

**Room 109 Independent Study
Final Product**

Name   Renae H.   **Class Period**   Silver D

Phone   555-8363   **Grade in School**   Senior

Title of Project   A Concerned Attempt with Sivvy

Partner   None

Two- to three-sentence description: an analysis of the relationship between Sylvia and Ted and Sylvia versus the world

Reading accomplished (e.g., books, articles):
1. *Sylvia Plath and Ted Hughes* by Margaret Uroff
2. The journals & poetry of Sylvia Plath
3. Letters home
4. Article: "The Triumph of a Tormented Poet"
5. Article: "Some God Got Hold of Me"
6. Newspaper clippings: "Hunt for Missing Smith Honor Student who left on 'long hike' Fruitless"; "Carry on Search for Plath Girl"; "Found at Home, Smith Senior in Fair Condition"; "Condition Good of Smith Senior Who Took Pills."
7. Article: "Two Poets Nourished Each Other's work— In Life and Death."
8. Short Story: As a Baby-sitter Sees It
9. Article: "The Sylvia Plath Forum"
10. Article: "Ted Hughes Breaks Silence over Sylvia Plath"
11. Article: "The Good Father"
12. Article: "The Literary Love Affair That Turned to Tragedy"
13. Poetry from Ariel, the Collosus, the Lupercal, Crossing the Water, and Wodwo
14. www.geocities.com/~emily777/PlathLinks.ht

Writing accomplished: **1.** 10-page paper on the relationship between Sivvy & Ted
2. 40 journal entries

In-school activities: Internet use, reading time, note taking, journal writing, talking to your English professor friend. I will paint a Hughes' poem on the wall next to the 109 door.

Out-of-school activities: Trip to Smith College, public library, Internet use, tons of reading, journal writing, thinking

Final Presentation of Project will include: A visual presentation and an explanation show how Sivvy's and Ted's relationship worked and did not work. A reading of my work and theirs; a talk on going to the archives at Smith College.

Anything more in your Independent Study portfolio?   I also read "Don't Sweat the Small Stuff"; "Trainspotting"; and "The Notebook."

Assess your performance: Below Average/Average/Honors/High Honors
I've worked seriously and probably deserve an honors or high honors grade. I really know Sivvy's life and work.

Figure 4–1. Renae's Final Product Form

The Freed Disciple of an Angel of Buddha

The Wilderness came as Buddha last night,
high on sex, its mouth full of smiling gods.
Running with his angels, I became their disciple,
electric and wild.
In sleep I meditate sadness, in sleep I am clothed.
I'm an explosion at dawn.
The heat is a moor in which I roam, roam, roam my
stringed limp figure—
The heat from my wilderness and my angels,
the heat and the Buddha and his magnified gods,
A face I have been staring into for too long,
Imagining freedom.
Lay me in the sea and tell me about your freedom.

After each student presents, I write a letter response to be included at the front of the ISP portfolio. The following is my final assessment letter to Renae, who had been my student for two years:

The Final Quarter
Room 109

Dear Renae,

And so the final words. Your interest in ideas is profound. Your understanding of poetry and poets is mature and thoughtful and far reaching. This was never more evident than when you spoke with Dr. Tom Newkirk of UNH. You impressed him. You made me proud. I see a brilliant future in all of this for you, Renae. This final quarter you have outgrown yourself.

Knowing you as a poet is a privilege. I suspect you will find your path and venture far with words. You are a wordsmith—you know how to invent and draw and look far beyond the physical world. This ability of meshing the earthbound with the metaphysical is a gift of the highest order. Your words take us soaring; they transcend what anyone would expect of a high schooler.

I look forward to hearing of your many successes in the world beyond Room 109. Don't take second best out *there*, Renae. Work at your craft, take no shortcuts, and you will help many of us see more clearly. Working with you has been a privilege.

"Farewell, fair spirit. Fare forward, voyager."

Always, Your Loving English Teacher,
Rich Kent

5

Career ISP

The meaning of our work, as Eisner reminds us, is in the lives it enables others to lead.

Jeffrey D. Wilhelm
You Gotta BE the Book

Kristin's Story: Mind/Body/Spiritual Healing

"I liked the way I learned more about myself from this project. I am happier."

During Kristin's ISP, she immersed herself in the study of healing alternatives. This junior in high school sees herself studying and practicing alternative medicine once she leaves high school. From therapeutic massage to Reiki (pronounced *ray kee*, a Japanese word for universal life energy), she entered the fascinating world of healers who integrate the power of the mind, body, and spirit to help people maintain the highest level of personal health.

As part of her independent study project, Kristin attended an evening class for women called "Increasing Your Energy." The class met once a week for a four weeks at a medical center some forty miles from her home. Kristin discussed spirituality, health, and alternative medicine with an Auyurvedic doctor, a priest, and a Reiki master. She spent forty-five minutes talking with the Reiki therapist and then took a one-hour massage that included aroma therapy.

For her ISP, Kristin read six books, wrote a twenty-page paper plus a series of book reviews, and drew a picture of the human body that included the various energy paths. Perhaps the most interesting product of her ISP was a finely crafted scrapbook of her various experiences. She included photographs, quotations, and personal writings. Her presentation to class lasted fifteen minutes and all of us had an opportunity to page through her collection.

This career ISP helped shape Kristin's life journey—a journey, I am sure, that will be filled with joy.

Ben's Story: Teaching Little People

By his sophomore year in high school Ben had convinced himself he would become an attorney. But after a few days in Mrs. Kellogg's third-grade class, he had found his calling.

During his ISP on elementary education, Ben rarely came to English class. He spent every free period at St. John's Elementary School working as a teacher assistant. At the beginning of his time with the children, Mrs. Kellogg asked each of her twenty-five third graders to write "Mr. Belanger" a letter (see Figure 5–1). In response, Ben wrote each student a letter (see Figure 5–2).

Also during his stay, Ben kept a daily log of his experiences. These journal entries gave me a good picture of his day-to-day work in the third grade; they also showed me that Ben will make a wonderful elementary school teacher with a great sense of humor.

The following is his first entry:

Day 1

Today is day one of my independent study. When I arrived at St. John's today the kids greeted me with cheers of "Hello, Mr. Belanger." This was weird. Imagine twenty-five people who you have never seen before being nice to you. During the kids' recess I talked with Mrs. Kellogg. She explained that the kids were told to respect me. She then proceeded to tell me what would be going on that day in her class. As recess culminated we went inside. Then we sat in a circle. I started by introducing myself. (Stage 109 all over again.) Everyone of them, forty-six eyes on me. I almost felt like the president at his inaugural address. Then the class went around in a circle and read me letters about themselves that they had written. I later took these letters and wrote personal reactions to all of the kids. Then the class did a math lesson. We played a game. To make sure that nobody was left out we chose groups from a basket. This was a great idea because you get to work with all different types of people. Even if you do not like certain people, it teaches you to work with different kinds. In life, you do not always work with people who you want to. What amazes me so much is the excitement level of kids. No matter what they are doing whether large or small it is appealing to them.

As part of his study, Ben went to the middle school to see how he would enjoy that age group. It didn't take him long to discover elementary school was where he belonged. "Those kids are wild," he said.

He also attempted a pen pal exchange between his English class and Mrs. Kellogg's students. After trying for ten days to make this happen, he real-

> Tuesday 4, 4.98
> room . 3.
>
> Dear Mr. Belanger,
>   My name is Maegin Jolin
>
> I have som things to tell you
> 1. I love gymnastics 2. I love
> reading 3. I love to do wrestling
> at grcc 4. and one inportent
> thing I never told you
> is that I love the teacher
> I have right know!
>
> # Mrs.Kellogg!!!!!!!!
>
>   your friend
>   Maegin

Figure 5–1. *Third-grader Maegin Jolin Welcomes ISP Student "Mr. Belanger"*

Dear Maegin,

Hello, my name is Benjamin Edward Belanger. I am a junior at Mountain Valley High School. I am currently in Mr. Kent's English class. For the next seven weeks I will be visiting your third grade classroom. The reason for this is that I plan to go to college to become a teacher. I enjoy working with young children. I am interested in how Mrs. Kellogg teaches you your subjects.

I am glad to see that you are doing journals already. When you get to high school you will be doing these all the time, so practicing them now will be very helpful. The revision process that Mrs. Kellogg is teaching you is very important. Some of Mr. Kent's students do up to ten revisions on one single paper. The geography lessons that you are doing will be very helpful, too.

You like gymnastics. My sister Elizabeth does too. She is not on a team. Are you? Most girls don't like wrestling. I had three girls on my basketball traveling team at the GRCC (community center). Those girls got a lot of experience by playing with the boys. They are really good players now on the high school team.

Reading is an important subject. You can learn a lot by reading. Wait until the high school teachers find out that you like to read. Do you like to write about what you read? In Mr. Kent's class we call this reflection. We write a lot about what we read and think.

Your teacher is a good teacher. That is why I chose to come to your class. I can see why you love her so much.

I hope to get to know you better!

Your friend,

Mr. Belanger

Figure 5–2. Ben Belanger's Letter to Third-grader Maegin Jolin

ized he had begun too late in the quarter and the exchange never got into full swing.

For his portfolio Ben wrote the following papers, each around one thousand words long: "Public School versus Private Schools"; "Stage 109 Is Over, Ya Right!"; and "Personal Reaction to Room 109." He also wrote a thank-you letter to Mrs. Kellogg and, as mentioned above, twenty-five letters to "his" students and a series of classroom observation journals.

During his ISP he read *You Can't Say You Can't Play* by Vivian Paley, *Room 109: The Promise of a Portfolio Classroom* by Richard Kent, *Dumbing Us Down* John Taylor Gatto, "On Telling the Story of Learning" by Michael Armstrong (unpublished article), "Listening to What Children Say" by Vivian Gussin Paley, *Walk on the Wild Side* by Dennis Rodman, *Rock This!* by Chris Rock. The last two books listed were unrelated to his independent study project. He chose them for pleasure reading.

Ben's ISP presentation to the class revealed his passion for teaching. For his ISP he received a high honors grade of 96. And in my final letter of the year to him, I ended with the following:

> You have made a difference in the lives of 25 little people at a small school up the road . . . and you have made a difference right here in Room 109 for me and for others. I wish you well. Congratulations, Ben.

Searching Out Careers

Part of my responsibility as a teacher is to stimulate my students' thinking about the careers they might like to enter. Whenever I'm teaching something like letter writing or interview techniques, relating that instruction to the outside world of work is important. Students must see the connection between their classroom studies and their future occupations.

Our high school's guidance department has a ton of career material, the most helpful of which is the *Occupational Outlook Handbook* published by the U.S. Department of Labor, Bureau of Labor Statistics. This 532-page book lists as many as two thousand jobs while highlighting important and interesting information concerning hundreds of various occupations. I borrow this book for a few weeks each year; it is by far the most popular item in class at the time. Kids enjoy dreaming and scheming about their futures while reading about the reality of certain jobs.

Let's say a student is interested in becoming a flight attendant. The *Occupational Outlook Handbook* gives a two-page overview of the occupation. Such information can grab a student's attention (check out the starting pay in 1996). The following is a condensed version:

Flight Attendants

Significant Points

- Job duties are learned through extensive formal training after being hired.
- The opportunity for travel attracts many to this career, but this occupation requires working nights, weekends, and holidays and frequently being away from home.

Nature of Work

- Major airlines are required by law to provide flight attendants for the safety of the flying public. Although the primary job of the flight attendant is to ensure that safety regulations are adhered to, they also try to make flights comfortable and enjoyable for passengers . . . .

Working Conditions

- Since airlines operate around the clock year round, flight attendants may work at night and on holidays and weekends. They usually fly 75 to 85 hours a month and in addition generally spend about 75 to 85 hours a month on the ground preparing planes for flights, writing reports following completed flights, and waiting for planes to arrive. . . .

Employment

- Flight attendants held about 132,000 jobs in 1996.

Training, Other Qualifications, and Advancement

- Airlines prefer to hire poised, tactful, and resourceful people who can interact comfortably with strangers and remain calm under duress. Applicants usually must be at least 19 to 21 years old. Flight attendants must have excellent health and the ability to speak clearly. In addition, there are height requirements and applicants should not have visible tattoos. Applicants must be high school graduates. Those having several years of college or experience in dealing with the public are preferred . . . .

Job Outlook

- Opportunities should be favorable for persons seeking flight attendant jobs . . . Those with at least 2 years of college and experience in dealing with the public should have the best chance of being hired . . . .

Earnings

- Beginning flight attendants had median earnings of about $12,800 a year in 1996, according to data from the Association of Flight Attendants. Flight attendants with 6 years of flying experience had a median annual earnings of about $19,000, while some senior flight attendants earned as much as $40,000 a year . . . .

Related Occupations

- Other jobs that involve helping people as a safety professional while requiring the ability to be pleasant even under trying circumstances include emergency medical technician, firefighter, maritime crew, and camp counselor.

Sources of Additional Information

- Information about job opportunities in a particular airline and the qualifications required may be obtained by writing to the personnel manager of the company.

In the handbook many charts and tables stimulate my students' thinking. One of the tables that I photocopy and hand out highlights the "Fastest growing occupations and occupations having the largest numerical increase in employment, projected 1996–2006, by level of education and training" (see Figure 5–3). As you will see, the table is divided into two sections, "Fastest growing occupations" and "Occupations having the largest numerical increase in employment." Thinking in these terms is important for sixteen-year-olds.

One of the handbook's charts (see Figure 5–4 on page 78) highlights the top twenty-five occupations with fast growth, high pay, and low unemployment. Interestingly, eighteen of those occupations require at least a bachelor's degree. The occupations are also rather concentrated, with five occupations in computer technology, four in health care, and five in education. Again, having our students think in these terms seems important.

To access the *Occupational Outlook Handbook* and much more via the Internet, visit the Web site at <http://stats.bls.gov/emphome.html>.

For those many students who are struggling with their futures, job assessment sheets can be helpful. Virtually every career book will have some sort of job conditions sheet like Figure 5–5 (page 79) from the Peterson's Guides series *Getting Skilled, Getting Ahead* (Myers and Scott 1989). After students go through the checklist, I find it helpful if they journal a bit before we talk about their ideas.

Other suggestions to stimulate your students' thinking about careers:

- Invite in your school's guidance people to talk about career choices.
- Click on to Yahoo, AltaVista, or any Internet search engine. Type in "Careers." What happens next is an explosion of job possibilities.
- Search commercial sites such as Jobs.com to help students see what the demands are.

Fastest growing occupations	Education/training category	Occupations having the largest numerical increase in employment
	First-professional degree	
Chiropractors		Lawyers
Veterinarians and veterinary inspectors		Physicians
Physicians		Clergy
Lawyers		Veterinarians and veterinary inspectors
Clergy		Dentists
	Doctoral degree	
Biological scientists		College and university faculty
Medical scientists		Biological scientists
College and university faculty		Medical scientists
Mathematicians and all other mathematical scientists		Mathematicians and all other mathematical scientists
	Master's degree	
Speech-language pathologists and audiologists		Speech-language pathologists and audiologists
Counselors		Counselors
Curators, archivists, museum technicians		Psychologists
Psychologists		Librarians, professional
Operations research analysts		Operations research analysts
	Work experience plus bachelor's or higher degree	
Engineering, science, and computer systems managers		General managers and top executives
Marketing, advertising, and public relations managers		Engineering, science, and computer systems managers
Artists and commercial artists		Financial managers
Management Analysts		Marketing, advertising, and public relations managers
Financial managers		Artists and commercial artists
	Bachelor's degree	
Data base administrators and computer support specialists		Systems analysts
Computer engineers		Teachers, secondary school
Systems analysts		Data base administrators and computer support specialists
Physical therapists		Teachers, special education
Occupational therapists		Computer engineers

Figure 5–3. Fastest Growing Occupations and Occupations Having the Largest Numerical Increase in Employment

Associate degree

Paralegals	Registered nurses
Health information technicians	Paralegals
Dental hygienists	Dental hygienists
Respiratory therapists	Radiologic technologists and technicians
Cardiology technologists	Health information technicians

Postsecondary vocational training

Data processing equipment repairers	Licensed practical nurses
Emergency medical technicians	Automotive mechanics
Manicurists	Medical secretaries
Surgical technologists	Emergency medical technicians
Medical secretaries	Hairdressers, hairstylists, and cosmetologists

Work experience

Food service and lodging managers	Clerical supervisors and managers
Teachers and instructors, vocational education and training	Marketing and sales worker supervisors
Lawn service managers	Food service and lodging managers
Instructors, adult education	Teachers and instructors, vocational education and training
Nursery and greenhouse managers	Instructors, adult (nonvocational) education

Long-term training and experience (more than 12 months of on-the-job training)

Desktop publishing specialists	Cooks, restaurant
Flight attendants	Correction officers
Musicians	Musicians
Correction officers	Police patrol officers
Producers, directors, actors, and entertainers	Carpenters

Moderate-term training and experience (1 to 12 months of combined on-the-job experience and informal training)

Physical and corrective therapy assistants and aides	Medical assistants
Medical assistants	Instructors and coaches, sports and physical training
Occupational therapy assistants and aides	Social and human services assistants
Social and human services assistants	Dental assistants
Instructors and coaches, sports and physical training	Physical and corrective therapy assistants

Short-term training and experience (up to 1 month of on-the-job experience)

Personal and home care aides	Cashiers
Home health aides	Salespersons, retail
Amusement and recreation attendants	Truck drivers, light and heavy
Adjustment clerks	Home health aides
Bill and account collectors	Teacher aides and educational assistants

Figure 5–3. (Continued)

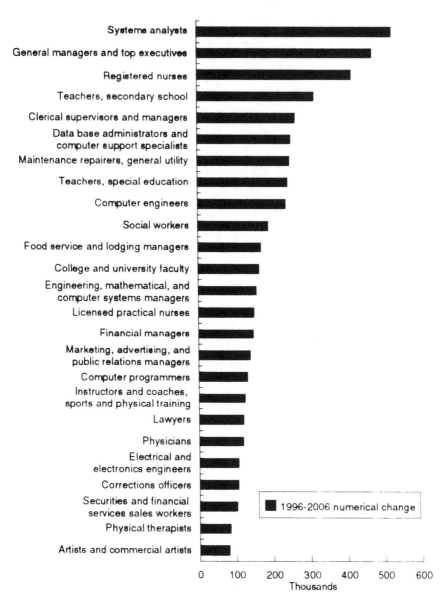

Figure 5–4. The Twenty-five Occupations with Fast Growth, High Pay, and Low Employment

WORK VALUES EXERCISE

Assess your opinion of the following job conditions.
Mark the box that best describes your feelings.

	Very Important	Somewhat Important	Not Important
Work near your home			
Work within an hour of home			
Work for a small company			
Work for a large company			
Work outdoors			
Work indoors			
Be physically active			
Work at a desk			
Work with others			
Work alone			
Be a part of a team			
Compete with others			
Be given work and directions			
Work independently			
Do same things each day			
Have a variety of tasks			
Be recognized for achievements			
Help others			
Make a good profit			

Figure 5–5. Work Values Exercise Focused on Job Conditions

- Click on to Amazon.com or any other Internet bookseller and type in "Career Books." Just reading the blurbs is interesting.
- Invite the local job services manager to talk with students.
- Encourage *all* students to take the Armed Services Vocational Aptitude Battery (ASVAB). This is a multi-aptitude test that measures potential for success in different jobs. This test is open to all high school students and does not mean they have to sign up for the armed services!
- Urge students to use career programs on computer (e.g., "Choices" created by Careerware, phone 1.800.267.1544). Students are systematically led through interest and skills' surveys to help them connect to a variety of occupations. "Choices" is an engaging program for young adults.
- Talk about the various post–high school options and the careers available. See Figure 5–6 for the careers available for the various levels of education.
- Urge students to look through *Military Careers: A Guide to Military Occupations and Selected Military Career Paths* published by the U.S. Department of Defense.
- Introduce other career books such as *Federal Jobs in Law Enforcement* edited by Russ Smith, *100 Best Careers for Writers and Artists* by Shelly Field, and *100 Jobs in Technology* by Lori Hawkins.
- Have students make a list of jobs they have considered. Share the list in class. I share my career history, too. In fact, I have photographs of the "other Mr. Kents" hanging in my classroom. They include Mr. Kent as a nineteen-year-old police officer, an Army cadet, a ski bum, a writer, a U.S. Space and Rocket Center trainee, a ski-soccer-lacrosse-track-biking coach, and of course, a teacher.

Having career books in the classroom offers students many opportunities to plan, scheme, and most important of all to dream. Chatting with students about their future lives gives me a connection well beyond my everyday teacher role. This connection makes my days in the classroom much more meaningful.

Searching Out Careers 81

Community college

accounting
architectural drafting
art
automotive technology
business administration
business management
civil engineering technology
computer & information systems
court reporting
dental assisting/dental hygiene
dietetics & nutrition
drafting
drama/theater
early childhood education
electronics engineering technology
executive assistant/secretary
fashion design
fashion merchandising
finance & banking
fire science/fire fighting
hotel/restaurant management
industrial engineering technology
journalism
law enforcement/police science
legal assisting/paralegal
marketing
mechanical engineering technology
medical administrative assisting
medical lab technology
music
nursing
occupational therapy assistant
physical therapist assistant
radiological technology
registered nurse
real estate
respiratory therapy
social work
travel & tourism
welding

Career and technical schools

accountant/bookkeeper
air conditioning/refrigeration
artist, commercial

auto body technician
barber/hairstylist
broadcaster
building trades
carpenter
child care
computer operator/programmer
computer service technician
cosmetologist
court reporter
data entry
dental assistant
dental laboratory technician
drafting
electrician
electronics
fashion designer
fashion merchandiser
flower arranger
heavy equipment operator
hotel-motel manager
interior designer
legal assistant/paralegal
legal secretary
licensed practical nurse
massage therapist
medical assistant
medical/dental receptionist
medical lab technician
medical secretary
motorcycle mechanic
nurse's aide
paperhanger
photographer
plumber
respiratory therapist
secretary
surveyor
tool-and-die maker
travel & tourism
truck driver
upholsterer
veterinarian assistant
welder
word processing

Figure 5–6. Careers Available for Various Levels of Education

Four-year colleges

accounting
anthropology
architecture
art education
art history
biology
botany
business administration
chemical engineering
chemistry
civil engineering
computer science
criminal justice
dance
drama
economics
electrical engineering
elementary education
English
environmental studies
finance
fine arts
French
geography
geology
German
history
home economics
information sciences
international relations
journalism
management
management/information systems
marketing
mathematics
mechanical engineering
music
music education
music performance
nursing
occupational therapy
pharmacy
philosophy
physical education
physical therapy
physics

political science
pre-med
pre-law
psychology
public relations
religion
secondary education
social work
sociology
Spanish
special education
speech pathology
urban studies
wildlife management
zoology

The military
Almost all civilian occupations can be found in the military service. In fact, the military service offers training and employment in over 2000 job specialties, 75 percent of which have civilian counterparts.

Apprenticeships
auto mechanic
bricklayer and stone mason
carpenter
cook
electrician
firefighter
machinist
painter & paperhanger
plumber
roofer
sheet-metal worker
tool-and-die maker

Immediate employment
Many businesses are anxious to find employees who are hard-working, polite, punctual, well-groomed, willing to learn, and able to get along well with others. If a person has a skill or talent in, for example, art, sales, or computers, that person can be quite valuable to an employer. Entry-level jobs in department stores, fast-food outlets, and the like offer an "in" for some students.

Figure 5–6. (Continued)

6

Hobby/Life Passion ISP

When the red Geo pulled into my driveway for our trip to the fish hatchery, I realized how great independent studies are. You study what is interesting to you and what you want to learn about. It is sort of like college, only better. You don't have to pay for books and tuition.

                                                              Ryan Parent, a junior

It's late May.

Nathan and Ryan haul their large, flat-bottomed canoe through the hallways of Mountain Valley High School. They built the boat over three consecutive weekends while Nathan's girlfriend, Rachel, videotaped the entire process. The boat is one part of their ISP "Gone Fishing."

We gather around the boat in the hallway outside our classroom. People are quiet; they can't believe what the boys have accomplished. I don't like admitting it now, but Nathan and Ryan had done so much throughout their last quarter that part of me wondered whether they had actually built this boat during ISP. The video did not lie.

You should know that I don't feel guilty for my skepticism. I've worked with teenagers for almost twenty-five years. My experience as a teacher tells me that during ISP I must be vigilant when it comes to work presented. I always look for drafts, and I demand work in progress. Quite simply, I stay involved and try my best to keep track.

Nathan and Ryan fished all over western Maine, in lakes and rivers and streams. They cast their lines on weekends and in the evening following school sports. They visited fish hatcheries and animal farms; they talked with game wardens at a road block and a licensed Maine Guide. Ryan joined the Mountain Valley High School Fishing Club and hung out with our resident fishing authority, John Bell, a special education teacher who still works summers for L. L. Bean.

What pleased me most about Nathan and Ryan's project was their level of commitment. Along with their flat-bottomed canoe and a video of its production, their final presentation included a video of their fishing expeditions, forty-eight photographs, an explanation of fishing equipment, posters of fishing facts, and a series of maps they had drawn. The talk lasted thirty minutes and sang loudly of the boys' love of fishing and the out-of-doors.

Along with his side trips, fishing expeditions, and boat building, Ryan created a portfolio which included the following:

- a 4-page paper on fishing in the Webb River
- a 4-page paper on visiting the animal farm and fish hatchery
- a 4-page paper on fly fishing with Mr. Bell
- two 1-page responses to fishing articles
- two 3-page responses to two fishing books
- twenty 1-page journal entries most were about fishing adventures

Nathan's portfolio included a rich collection of experience, too. His "Final Product" sheet is seen in Figure 6–1.

Letters: Telling the Story of Independent Study Projects

In response to their ISP portfolios, each student receives a *keeper* letter, two letters from fellow students, and a letter from me. These letters help my students see their projects from a variety of sides.

The following is one paragraph from my one-and-a-half page letter response of Ryan's independent study project and portfolio:

> I'm proud of you for your fishing project. Not only did you read and write, but you created, through geometry and technology, a stunning symbol of your work in the form of that flat-bottomed canoe. The videos and the organization of your presentation was solid. All in all, this is a project that I will brag about in the future. Tomorrow's 109ers will admire your work, but dislike you for the standards you set! Ha! Let them suffer.

I ask the adults in my students' lives to offer their thinking on the students' ISP. These *keeper* letters are often quite amazing for their honesty. Nathan's parents were a bit dubious about his plan—especially the boat-building part—but they supported him. The following is his mother's portfolio letter:

> June 2
>
> Dear Mr. Kent,
>
> This has been a really busy quarter for Nathan. When he came home from school and told us about what he was going to do for his English project

**Room 109 Independent Study
Final Product**

Name   Nate Cushman   **Class Period**   Silver A

Phone   555-9409   **Grade in School**   Junior

Title of Project   GONE FISHING

Partner(s)   Ryan Parent

Two- to three-sentence description   Gone Fishing is our lifelong experience and de-sire to do research and to learn how to catch the BIG ONES. Also to fulfill our lifelong dream and build our own canoe.

Reading accomplished (e.g., books, articles) :
    1. *The Old Man and the Sea*
    2. *Fishing with Hemingway and Glassell*
    3. *Nature I Loved*
    4. Many articles from *Outdoor Life*—in portfolio
    5. Articles from *Maine Fishing & Wildlife*—in portfolio

Writing accomplished: All papers are at least 3 pages long with at least 3 edits
    1. Paper on trip to Gray Animal Farm
    2. Paper on Fishing Facts
    3. Paper on Fishing Experiences with Ryan
    4. Reaction to *The Old Man and the Sea*
    5. Reaction to *Fishing with Hemingway and Glassell*
    6. 20 Fishing trip journals

In-school activities: Made 2 maps of the Rangeley Lakes Region and of Baxter State Park—read 15–20 articles from *Maine Fishing & Wildlife* magazine, *Outdoor Life*—typed up my animal farm trip paper—*The Old Man and the Sea* paper—wrote ten journals—talked to Mr. Bell about fly fishing.

Out-of-school activities: Fished Webb River once, Rangeley River once, beaver Pond seven times, Mooselookmeguntic twice, Garland Pond twice, Rangeley Lake three times, Androscoggin River three times—visited Rangeley Fish Hatchery, New Gloucester State Fish Hatchery, Gray Animal Farm—made a 6-minute video, took 48 pictures, talked to Fred Martineau a licensed guide—stopped at a game warden's road block—made a flat bottomed canoe and took 30 minutes of video over the three weekends we made it on.

Final Presentation of Project will include: Present 48 pictures—present both maps—show fishing video—tell information from the guide—show lures—present poster of interesting fishing facts—present and clean a fish—tell about the warden's road block—bring in trophy bass—show canoe and canoe video. 30 minute presentation.

Anything more in your Independent Study portfolio?

Reactions to articles I found interesting—5 of them.

Assess your performance: Below Average/Average/Honors/High Honors

HIGH HONORS.

Figure 6–1. Nathan's Final Product Form

we had some doubt that he could build a boat. But his father said we'd give him the money to do it anyway. He worked on his project every day in between playing baseball and practices he even found the time to go fishing and get other things done that he needed. I am so proud of his accomplishments and the way he proved us to be wrong.

Brenda C.

I ask students to read and respond to other Room 109 students' work. We do these peer readings from 9 A.M. to noon on Saturday and Sunday mornings at the end of the quarter. Kelley volunteered as a student reviewer and wrote Ryan this thoughtful letter response one Sunday morning in school:

Dear Ryan Parent,

You've done a really nice job on your portfolio. I am impressed. You are definitely a writer. Your first paper, Webb River Fishing, was neat. I can picture you out there with your grandfather trying to catch a big fish and laughing when all you get is a little one. You still had a few typos/errors in your final draft. Watch out for those.

Three Dollars was a funny story. I can hear you in this one. I had to laugh out loud a couple of times. These is one really long paragraph. I'm sure you could have broken it up easily. I like this paper the most.

It sounds like the fishing club is a lot more fun than you'd think. I wish more people weren't too cool to be in the fishing club. I'm sure a lot of people would have a lot of fun. I'm glad you enjoyed yourself with it. This paper was interesting because you've included all the characters. Nice work.

I can really tell you had a great time with your independent study project. You have picked the right subject. Keep writing Ryan. You do a wonderful job.

Kelley P.

Each volunteer reader receives extra credit added directly onto their quarter-end grade. Normally, I assign two points when a student reads three portfolios and writes three, 1-page letter responses. About thirty student readers are lured in by this extra-credit incentive.

In this time of respecting multiple intelliegences, I am not sure if "average student" is an acceptable term. However, for lack of a better expression, Nathan and Ryan are average students who performed extraordinarily. Each received a high honors assessment while repeating, almost word-for-word, "This is the most fun I've had in school."

When I spoke with the boys about this year's ISP, Ryan had decided that he would be studying mountain bikes with his buddy Devin. As for Nathan, he is thinking about building a log cabin with two other friends. The three will construct it, they hope, in the woods out back of the high school where Room 109 maintains a poetry garden near a small stream. They will find out right off, I suspect, that building a log cabin is one tough assignment. They also may discover that they are not up for the challenge. Whatever happens, though, they will learn.

Suggested Hobbies

Click on to any search engine on your computer; on or near the front page is a section called something like "Hobbies and Interests." From there, as always, the world opens up.

Figure 6–2 is a list of hobbies, interests, or life passions that help my students inventory their own interests while looking at possible ISPs.

action figures
arts and crafts
amateur and ham radio
amateur telescope making
angels
antiques
aquariums
astrology
astronomy
autographs
aviation
backgammon
basketry
beading
Beanie Babies
beekeeping
bell ringing
birding
blacksmithing
board games
books
candle making
cartooning
cats
ceramics/pottery
checkers
chess
clay figures
clocks
collecting
currency
decoupage
diplomacy
dolls
dream analysis
dressmaking
electronics
embroidering
fantasy baseball
film and TV memorabilia

filmmaking
fish
flower arranging
food and cooking
games
gardening
genealogy
ghosts
glass crafts
gold panning
guitar making
health
heraldry
historical reenactment
horoscopes
improvisations
juggling
kites
knitting
knotting
lock picking
magazines
magic and illusions
metal detecting
miracles
models (e.g., planes, trains)
nautical
needlework
Nostradamus
numerology
origami
painting
paper crafts
papermaking
paranormal
pets
photography
pottery
puppetry
quilting

radio
radio controlled vehicles
railways
retrocollecting
riddles and puzzles
rockets
rocks, gems, minerals
role playing
roller blading
rug making
Scrabble
scrapbooks
sewing
sewing machines
snow mobiling
soapmaking
sport memorabilia
Star Trek
Star Wars
stenciling
string figures
Tarot
textiles
toy collecting/making
trading cards (e.g. baseball, football)
treasure hunting
tropical fish
typewriter collecting
UFOs/aliens
unicycling
urban exploration
vintage cars
water colors
wood burning
wood carving
writing
X-Files (TV show)

Figure 6–2. Hobbies, Interests, and Life Passions

7

Multitheme ISP

Some students have a number of interests and wish to combine two or three themes. For me, the key word here is "interests." At the risk of having the students perform surface work, I fall on the side of their interests. The following is one fine example.

Jason's Project:
Architecture, Nature, and Art

A repeat 109er, Jason had been thinking about his second ISP since summer time. His first independent study project on architecture and art showed all of us in class the potential of multithemed independent study projects. During this nine-week study at the end of his junior year, Jason job-shadowed an architect in a nearby city, built a scale model house, studied the work of Frank Lloyd Wright, kept an artistic journal, revised (fourteen times!) a poem about drawing, read parts of three art books, wrote a number of revealing essays, and presented an in-depth talk to his classmates on both architecture and art. Indeed, in his first ISP Jason performed as an emerging professional throughout this self-designed investigation.

When Jason wrote up his second ISP proposal, I simply said, "Go for it!" Two of the three themes—architecture, nature, and art—overlapped his first year's work; however, his activities in and out of the classroom would differ and so would his products. More important, since Jason planned to head off to college the next fall with hopes to study architecture and art, continuing his study made absolute sense.

During the course of his ISP, Jason trekked to Walden Pond, three-and-a-half hours away, in Concord, Massachusetts. There, he videotaped, photographed, and sketched. He also brought back a full collection of brochures and maps from the Walden Pond State Reservation and the Walden Conservancy. He placed these souvenirs in his portfolio; to complement his portfolio, he included a number of photographs he had snapped during his journey.

89

While in Massachusetts, Jason and his father toured a college with an architecture program. Further, he visited a prominent architectural firm to interview a number of architects. These few days proved important not only for the ISP but for thinking about his future.

Back at home, Jason painted and labeled a map of Walden Pond. He also crafted a wooden stand on which to display the 20- by 30-inch rendering. Finally, he placed the map beneath Plexiglas. This project sings of professionalism.

From one of his sketches at Walden, Jason painted in oils a cubist, Picassoesque representation of Thoreau's cabin. In his portfolio cover sheets he wrote, "This painting may very well have been my most successful project in my two years of 109 . . . It was a long process that ended with great satisfaction."

For the nature section of his ISP, Jason read portions of Henry David Thoreau's *Walden* as well as a selection of quotations by Thoreau in the *Hurricane Island Outward Bound Book of Readings*. From *Essays* by Ralph Waldon Emerson, he read "Nature," a challenging and sophisticated piece I copied for him. Reading a photocopy of "Nature" gave Jason an opportunity to practice highlighting vital points and jotting marginal notes. These reading and research skills are important for students, yet they are often neglected in my public school classroom.

For the next section of his ISP, Jason trucked off on a Saturday with his dad and brother to Rapid River. In the early to mid-1900s, the late author Louise Dickinson Rich (*We Took to the Woods, My Neck of the Woods*) made her home on the tumbling river. The area is rich with lakes and deep forests. Accessed by a series of secondary and gravel roads, Rapid River is about an hour's drive straight into the woods northwest of our town. Jason set up a tent and camped the night by himself. He videotaped, photographed, journaled, sketched, and hiked in the back country of Maine's western mountains.

As a result of his camping trip on Rapid River, Jason created another dazzling map encased in Plexiglas (Figure 7–1). He read *We Took to the Woods*, twelve chapters from *Nature I Loved* by Bill Geagan, and Maine's young adult classic *Lost on a Mountain in Maine* by Don Fendler.

For writing, Jason composed "Perfection: An essay on Architecture and Nature." This seven-page paper recounted his experiences in Massachusetts; he also explored his thinking while creating a picture of the harmony between the natural world and the world of humankind's creations. He writes, "In my community, buildings, houses, and other structures are sacred works of art, while trees, rivers, and ponds serve as natural wonders."

His hope for fifteen to thirty "new-level" journal entries never materialized. In his portfolio Jason included only eight, 150-word journals. In truth, he had spent so much time on other aspects of his ISP that journaling took a back seat.

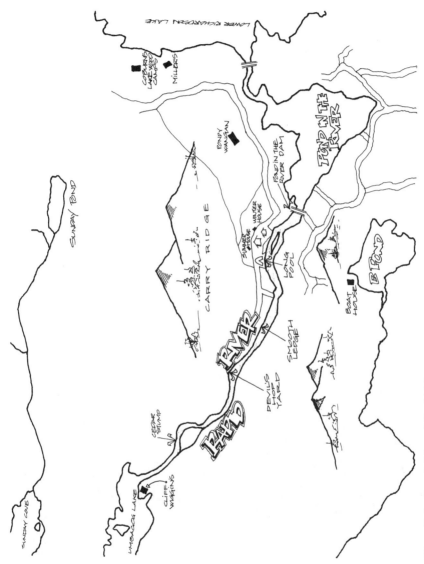

Figure 7–1. Jason's Map of Rapid River

One other writing project unrelated to his themes is the poem, "The Warrior." From early March through the beginning of May, Jason worked with me as his primary editor on this football poem celebrating his team and the mask he painted on his face prior to games. I guided him through eighteen drafts of the poem.

Near the end of his ISP time, Jason went back to his elementary school, St. John's Catholic School. He showed his artwork to the third-grade students and fielded questions from the little people.

For his final presentation at the end of May, Jason spoke for thirty-five minutes in Room 109. During his talk he showed two of his architectural drawings (see Figure 7–2). He had seen these houses during his ISP visits. He also passed around a foam board with a photo collage of his presentation at St. John's, his trip to Rapid River, and his visit to Massachusetts. By the time he had shown the videotape, his maps, and all of his other work, his classmates and I sat in awe.

Though Jason did not accomplish the amount of writing he had planned, I was compelled to award a high honors assessment. Jason opened our eyes to the power and potential of multithemed independent study projects. See Figure 7–3 for my final letter response.

Figure 7–2. One of Jason's Architectural Drawings

Saturday, May 31

Room 109

Dear Jason,

Last night you stopped by to deliver your final portfolio for Room 109. I must admit I felt sad. I'll miss you. From your kind and understated way to your brilliant artwork, you have graced this classroom and helped me understand even more the need for artistic expression in English class. You helped all of us "see" books and ideas from a place far away from the ordinary.

This past week you have amazed us yet again with your stunning artistic abilities. The architectural drawings of "your" house and the cubist painting of Thoreau's cabin; the beautifully crafted maps of Walden and Rapid River; the photo essay of your time teaching drawing to Mrs. K's third-grade class; and the video of your experiences at the architectural firm, Walden, and two days alone in the woods on Rapid River—this work, like all of your creations, touches excellence.

Moving on to Central Maine Technical College for a year or two seems to be just the right thing for you. Show them your stuff and they'll be as breathless as your classmates and I have been these past two years. From there, I know you'll *tear a hole in the sky!*

Jason, you have made a profound difference in Room 109, and you leave a lasting legacy. For that and so much more, you have my deepest gratitude and respect.

Always, YLET,
Richard Kent

If a man does not keep pace with his companions, perhaps it is because he hears a different drummer. Let him step to the music he hears, however measured or far away.

Henry David Thoreau

Figure 7–3. Kent's Final Letter Response to Jason

8

Selected Reading ISP

"I'd just like to read."

Graduating in a few months and expecting a child soon after, Tabitha knew that settling in with a series of books would be a good use of her time. So, she interviewed three teachers in our school and put together a list of books she thought she'd enjoy. Tabitha's Final Product form (see Figure 8–1) reveals the work she accomplished.

Throughout the last quarter of her senior year, Tabitha could be seen sitting in remote corners of the school reading a book. Week after week she immersed herself. She looked so relaxed—I envied her this opportunity to read and then to reflect on the books.

Some might argue that Tabitha needed to have a discussion group to help her discover a variety of levels to the literature. But this eighteen-year-old mom-to-be knew what she wanted—knew what she needed. At some point in school, and more frequently than not, I know I have to trust my students to make this kind of choice. I'm not sure that a selected reading ISP is the correct choice for some of my students. They need a more varied English menu. In Tabitha's case, however, this project was just what the doctor ordered.

And yes, mom and baby are just fine.

Selected Reading, Suggested Books

There are endless lists of suggested books from places such as the American Library Association, Booklist, the School Library Journal, Internet booksellers, the National Council of Teachers of English, or local libraries. The Internet offers sites focused on specific topic headings; type "Reading Lists" into your favorite search engine.

Other lists are available in such places as:

- *GRE Literature in English* by Pauline Beard, Ph.D. et al. Suggested reading list of literary works (Princeton, NJ, 1997, ix–xvii).

Room 109 Independent Study
Final Product

Name Tabitha Jones   **Class Period** Silver A

Phone 555-0261   **Grade in School** Senior

Title of Project Independent Reading Project

Partner(s) None

Two- to three-sentence description A look into books that have been deemed important by faculty members here at MVHS. They are books that offer lessons through both fiction and nonfiction stories.

Reading accomplished (e.g., books, articles):
1. *The Catcher in the Rye* by J.D. Salinger
2. *The Woman Warrior* by Maxine Hong Kingston
3. *A Separate Peace* by John Knowles
4. *Death Be Not Proud* by John Gunther
5. *The Grapes of Wrath* by John Steinbeck

Writing accomplished:
Edited reviews of:
1. *The Catcher in the Rye*, 3 pages, 7 drafts
2. *The Woman Warrior*, 3 pages, 6 drafts
3. *A Separate Peace*, 3 pages, 5 drafts
4. *Death Be Not Proud*, 3 pages, 4 drafts
5. 25 free journals; 10 book reaction journals

In-school activities: I spoke with several teachers (Mr. Sassi, Mr. Kiesman, Mrs. Peters) about important books to read. I spent the majority of my time typing, editing, reading, and writing journals.

Out-of-school activities: I read books, created projects, wrote journals, and typed.

Final Presentation of Project will include: Visual projects over 3 of the books I read. I will also discuss the value of each book.

Anything more in your Independent Study portfolio? I am giving the senior address. So I wrote it and had it edited by Ms. Wood. I also wrote a number of good-bye letters to teachers.

Assess your performance: Below Average/Average/Honors/High Honors

Average: I worked consistently and with an honorable amount of effort, but I was unable to complete everything I had intended.

Figure 8–1. Tabitha's Final Product Form

- National Book Foundation's Recommendations—The Foundation offered the following reading lists:

American History

Parting the Waters by Taylor Branch
The Unredeemed Captive by John Demos
Reconstruction by Eric Foner
Gunfighter by Richard Slotkin
Battlefield by Peter Svenson

Autobiography and Biography

Jefferson and Monticello by Jack McLaughlin
Anne Sexton by Diane Wood Middlebrook
Becoming a Man by Paul Monette
Jackson Pollock by Steven Naifeh and Gregory White Smith
Righteous Pilgrim by T. H. Watkins

Science and Nature

Danger and Survival by McGeorge Bundy
Silent Spring by Rachel Carson
Chaos by James Gleick
The Snow Leopard by Peter Matthiessen
No Nature by Gary Snyder

National Book Award Classics: The first 25 years

To Kill a Mockingbird by Harper Lee
A Good Man Is Hard to Find by Flannery O'Connor
The Catcher in the Rye by J.D. Salinger
Rabbit Redux by John Updike
Collected Earlier Poems by William Carlos Williams

- *Breathing In, Breathing Out: Keeping a Writer's Notebook* by Ralph Fletcher; References for writers' notebooks (Portsmouth, NH: Heinemann, 1996, 95–96)
- *Seeking Diversity: Language Arts with Adolescents* by Linda Rief: Recommended books for young adults, (Portsmouth, NH: Heinemann, 1992, 256–259)
- *It's Never Too Late* by Janet Allen: Recommended books for young adults, (Portsmouth, NH: Heinemann, 1995, 206-209)
- Arrowhead Library System "College Bound Reading List" can be found at: http://als.lib.wi.us/Collegebound.html

- Women's National Book Association has compiled a list titled "Eighty Books for 21st-Century Girls" found at: http://www.he.net/~susannah/wnba80books.html
- *100 Books for Girls to Grow On* by Shireen Dodson (1998)
- *Great Books for Boys: More Than 600 Books for Boys 2 to 14* by Kathleen Odean (1998).
- I'd also suggest an independent study project where students interview district staff members to gather a list of "must reads." The study could be further developed by having students go out in their community to discover what the community's "must reads" are. Compiling this list could be important for the local library, bookstores, the school district, and the community at large.
- Each year I collect a list of favorites from my students (see Figure 8–2). I post the list on my bookshelves. Reading these recommendations helps students select appropriate books. It's the old "If-he-read-it, I'd-like-to-try-it" syndrome. The same happens when students post their books on our "Books of 109" computer site, as mentioned earlier in this book.

Recommended Books
from *109ers*

Book   Author   Recommended by:
Into the Wild   (Jon Krackauer)   Aaron Gagnon
    AWESOME book . . . a young man's search for freedom in the wilderness

Into Thin Air   (Jon Krakauer)   Rich Kent
    INCREDIBLE book . . . the tragic ascent of Mt. Everest in 1996

Blind Courage   (Bill Irwin)   Rich Kent
    A blind man hikes the Appalachian Trail with his dog

An Unquiet Mind   (Kay Redfield Jamison)   Kim Theriault
    The look into a unique life and mind

Way of the Peaceful Warrior   (Dan Millman)   Melissa Thibodeau
    A young man, an athlete, discovers himself

Climbing Back   (Mark Wellman)   Brian Arsenault
    A paraplegic ranger who climbs El Capitan

She's Come Undone   (Wally Lamb)   Maia Dumas
    One of the most popular books of the year

A River Runs Through It   (Norman McLean)   E. J. Martin
    Brothers, fishing, life

Succulent Wild Women   (Sark)   Katie Doucette
    For girls and boys . . . on women

Relic   (Preston/Child)   Kurt Milligan
    A series of brutal murders in a New York museum

Robert Frost   (Jeffrey Meyers)   Matt Glazier
    The latest biography of the poet

Wherever You Go, There You Are   (Jon-Zabalt Zin)   Renae Hodgkins
    Coming to know yourself

The Book of Ruth   (Jane Hamilton)   Melissa Thibodeau
    The life pleasures of Ruth Grey

The Jungle   (Upton Sinclair)   Kate Austin
    A look into the Chicago meat packing plants

Angela's Ashes   (Frank McCourt)   Renae Hodgkins
    The life of an Irish boy

Figure 8–2. Favorite Books of Room 109

Girl, Interrupted   (Susana Kaysen)   Jess Fulton
   An 18-year-old girl's life in a psychiatric hospital

Fade   (Robert Cormier)   Rich Kent
   This teenager can become invisible

Right on the Edge of Crazy   (Mike Wilson)   Brooke Carey
   U.S. downhill ski team on the road & slopes

Ellen Foster   (Kaye Gibbons)   Monica Wood
   A foster girl comes to terms with life

The Giver   (Lois Lowry)   Everybody!
   A young boy lives a life in the future

The Writing Life   (Annie Dillard)   Everybody!
   A writer's journal . . . BRILLIANT

Jonathan Livingston Seagull   (Richard Bach)   Everybody!
   A not-so-ordinary seagull seeks new levels

Balm in Gilead   (Sara Lawrence Lightfoot)   Wendy Michaud
   The life of one of the first African-American women doctors

We Took to the Woods   (Louise Dickinson Rich)   Everybody!
   Life in the 1930s on the lakes near South Arm

Playing for Knight   (Steve Alfond)   Matt Carrier
   One basketball player's life with Bobby Knight

Einstein's Dreams   (Alan Lightman)   E. J. Martin
   Einstein's theories related in engaging short stories

This Boy's Life   (Tobias Wolff)   Jarod Richard
   One boy's life with a stepfather and interesting mother

Maus   (Art Speigleman)   Wendy Michaud
   Cartoon version of the Holocaust

Figure 8–2. (Continued)

9

Questions and Concerns

Throughout the course of independent study projects over the past years, and especially while writing this book, a number of questions have surfaced from teachers, administrators, and student teachers. I hope this section will clear up most of those questions. If not, drop me a line at Mountain Valley High School, Room 109, Hancock Street, Rumford, ME 04276.

If you were a beginning teacher, would you add ISP to your curriculum in your first or second year?
Yes and no. I would probably do a two- or three-week mini-ISP at the end of the year. My focus would be on the projects introduced at the beginning of this book. Projects that would get kids out of the classroom and then out of school.

What about the liability factor for kids leaving school?
Students' *keepers* and teachers must sign a school district prearranged absence form, included earlier in the book, when students leave school for any reason. Liability, therefore, is assumed by the parent/guardian. No signed form, no dismissal from school. Remember, too, *keepers* sign the ISP preliminary prospectus form.

Is it a problem amongst other staff if students miss class?
Some students miss one or two full days of school during the fourth quarter; others might miss four or five. Some plan their out-of-school work during the ninety minutes of their Room 109 time or their study halls. Still others, like Ryan and Nathan during their fishing ISP, never leave school; all of their ISP outside work was accomplished on weekends, after school, or over spring break.

Most of our faculty seem to be of a like mind when it comes to students missing school. The student is responsible for making up the work. I like to think of ISP as an adult experience. When we are absent from work or away from home, we work to make up what's not been done.

Have keepers (parent/guardians) ever refused to let their children leave school for an ISP adventure?
For the most part, *keepers* have been extraordinarily supportive of independent study projects. They are informed of the projects from the outset. However, if a child is struggling in mathematics, let's say, *keepers* are less likely to allow the child to miss that particular class. Likewise, if a child has been absent a great deal for other reasons (e.g., illness, sports, outside projects for other classes), *keepers* negotiate with their child and sometimes with me concerning future absences.

In seven years I haven't received a significant complaint about independent study projects from the adults in my students' lives. The typical "criticism" from *keepers* is, "Why didn't they have this kind of experience when I was in high school?"

What if a student has a similar independent experience going on in another class?
In fact, my friend Jerry Kiesman has his psychology students out in the community during fourth quarter as well. When we share a student, as we did with Sandra who worked with Alzheimer patients, we develop a combined experience that fulfills both class requirements. Communication is and always will be the answer. Typically, students create one larger portfolio to satisfy the requirements of both classes.

What if a student does not want to do an independent study project?
A few students opt out of ISP. They create a "regular old portfolio"; they have no energy for any of this creative stuff. For those students, fewer than ten per year, we agree on the themes for papers, and except for trips to the Writing Center, computer room, or media center, they will work in the classroom most of the time. Their portfolios still have a certain independent flavor to them. Although we do have class gatherings for minilessons and talks on people's ISP progress, I don't conduct many theme-based class discussions during fourth quarter. This means there is more decision making, time management, and independence for the students who choose the everyday portfolio.

Generally, kids who prefer to create a traditional portfolio do so for a couple of reasons. First, over the previous three quarters they have gained a certain amount of comfort and satisfaction in developing these books. They think, "I finally got the hang of this portfolio thing, and now he wants to change the rules." Second, the regular 109 portfolio and its freedom has stretched these students enough, and they know it. They're simply not ready for ISP, and I respect that.

What do community people say about ISP?
The overwhelming majority of people I have spoken with say that this experience for high school kids is invaluable. Certainly, from time to time ISP students perform poorly under certain circumstances, but this is all a part

of their learning. And one of my jobs is to address any of these shortcomings in terms that will help my students see their mistakes and work toward correcting them in the future.

We work hard to promote these projects in our community. Our students are properly prepared and each follow up a field experience with a thoughtful thank-you note. We talk extensively about making a good impression by working hard and about contacts—the students have heard me say more than once, "It's not always what you know, but who you know that lands you the job."

If you were a teacher with 150 or more students, would you run an independent study program? If so, how might you go about it?
Absolutely. I would partner with a local school of education and mentor two student teachers (a practice I am beginning this coming year). They would help with the management of ISP students, not to mention the mass of portfolio reading and responding. I would write a letter to my students' *keepers* and to re-tired teachers seeking volunteers. I would also write letters soliciting businesses and individuals in both the public and private sectors to take on ISP students.

I know this would be difficult, but I also know that this is an important program for students.

Do you ever have help managing ISP?
More and more I am soliciting help from Student Research Assistants. Because ISP goes through May and early June when colleges are out for summer break, I often have the luxury of help from former students. Most of my student research assistants are studying to become teachers and love the idea of coming in to help, whether they're paid or not.

If I have any "personal days" left—teachers in my district are afforded three per year—I hire a student to interview my present students or *keepers*. When I say hire, I mean they come in as a substitute teacher for the $55 per diem and their job is to do what I need done. When my personal days are gone, I pay the college student out of my own pocket. The results are worth the money. Finally, some students just want to be part of the action and are hanging out until their summer job begins. These young people don't care about making money.

Lincoln came in as a substitute and interviewed most of my students in mid-May. He took notes on their ISP progress and wrote a paragraph of observations for each student. The following is one he wrote for a multimedia program three students were developing about our English class:

WOW! This idea is so fantastic. I'm wicked excited about this. Just imagine all the things they are getting from this CD ROM project on Room 109. CDs are the future, computer programs are money making machines. These guys are on top of it all. I can't wait to see the end results. They're working well together.

He cheered some kids on and offered a variety of ideas to most. For those who were slacking, he delivered a few motivational words. To sum up his experience, Lincoln wrote a five-page observation of Room 109 independent study projects. The following is an excerpt:

Huh. I'm sitting at your desk. Incredible. I never thought I would be doing something like this four or five years ago. I had fun interviewing the students. Most of them have a good grasp on what they want to do. Some are lost and some are just lost to the end-of-the-year thoughts of summer and don't seem motivated . . .

One thing that scared me was those students who couldn't get going. I wonder if the freedom of such a project scared them? I wonder if they can handle it? Actually, I know they can, but I think it is a matter of letting go of structure and being confident in themselves. Some of these kids depend too much on being told what to do. They can not develop their own plans. They are stuck in the institution's trap . . .

Reading his observations helped me evaluate ISP and its importance. As a result of his fine work, I invited Lincoln to student teach here in Room 109. His four-month stint was, in a word, extraordinary.

Do kids ever take advantage of ISP? Do they fib about places they're going? Do they ever fail to show up for interviews or internship opportunities?
Of course.
I'm fond of saying that Room 109 is not Never-Never Land. Far from it. We're about learning and growing, and the best of this has blunders, failures, and restarts—sort of like any effective teaching practice or an IBM salesman's day trying to market million-dollar computer systems to companies that already have million-dollar computer systems. Furthermore, and I am not dismissing teenagers' indiscretions—sometimes young people get caught in a pickle and don't have the adult skills to escape—in other words, they mess up.
ISP can put students in whole-world situations that require real solutions. Just the other day, two boys signed out of school to go to the public library. They had the prearranged absence sheet filled—all was in order. I called the library to check on them. They never made it. McDonald's and a loop on back roads . . . the next Saturday morning they were in detention hall for truancy. Another lesson learned.

How do you assess independent study projects?
Once ISP portfolios are passed in, I read and respond to them over the last few weeks of school. Reading portfolios at this time of the year is less of a chore because I have finished my senior students' portfolios by the first week of June. I read underclasspeople's portfolios during the final two weeks of school. During one week, my students are working on their extensive final re-

flections of the year. During the second week, our school has final a examination period, and since I don't give final exams, my students have the time to work on their reflections while I push through with the remaining portfolios.

As always, students receive letters from their *keepers*, two students, and me. They also receive a two-page assessment sheet (see Figure 9–1). Together with the questions they are asked during their ISP presentation, these students are moved to consider their work in terms that will help them see the next level of accomplishment. In the end, the letters, assessment sheets, and presentation questions help my students see clearly themselves and their work.

Do students ever fail?
Yes.

Much is written about the value of failure, or what I call "guided failure." It might irk some people to hear that in a few instances I guide students to their demise in Room 109. That's right, I probably could prevent the failure, but in helping them pass I would take over too much of the student's responsibility. Truly, I know in my gut that a few of my kids need to fail this class.

In the "Biographical Note" of John Taylor Gatto's treatise *Dumbing Us Down: The Hidden Curriculum of Compulsory Schooling* (1992), I read the following: "People have to be allowed to make their own mistakes and try again, or they will never *master* themselves" (xiv). Mastering ourselves. Reinventing ourselves. This is life's work. And this is exactly what ISP allows and encourages.

Does Mountain Valley High School have a schoolwide independent study program?
We used to. In fact, I went through our school's independent study program as a senior. So did our local optometrist, a lawyer, some teachers, and an assistant at the local funeral parlor, to name a few.

During this week, first-year students participated in a drug and alcohol awareness program. Sophomores went through a career week. And with their homeroom advisers, juniors and seniors lined up week long independent study adventures both in and out of school.

I'd love to have Mountain Valley start up independent study weeks again. In fact, I feel the junior and senior students should spend most of their final high school years involved in apprenticeships or internships.

During the course of ISP, do you ever have full class discussions or minilessons?
Sure. And often. I schedule them, so all of the students know in advance. We talk about the progress of each student's ISP. These talks give other students ideas for their own projects. I frequently hear, "Gee, I want to do that." To which I reply, "Go for it!" These talks also help us make suggestions about a student's ISP. These catch-up sessions seem quite valuable.

Room 109 Assessment
Independent Study Projects

Name _____   Year in School _____

Class Period _____   Date _____

General

Evidence of Preparation:	Very Strong	Strong	OK	Weak
Work Ethic:	Very Strong	Strong	OK	Weak
Organization:	Very Strong	Strong	OK	Weak
Creativity:	Very Strong	Strong	OK	Weak
Depth of study:	Very Strong	Strong	OK	Weak
Work Completed Out of school:	Very Strong	Strong	OK	Weak
Contacts:	Very Strong	Strong	OK	Weak
Presentation:	Very Strong	Strong	OK	Weak

Reading

Difficulty:	Very Strong	Strong	OK	Weak
Amount:	Very Strong	Strong	OK	Weak
Variety:	Very Strong	Strong	OK	Weak

Projects

Interesting:	Very Strong	Strong	OK	Weak
Artistic:	Very Strong	Strong	OK	Weak
Time Spent:	Very Strong	Strong	OK	Weak

Figure 9–1. Final Assessment Forms

Journals

Interesting:	Very Strong	Strong	OK	Weak
Diverse:	Very Strong	Strong	OK	Weak
Amount:	Very Strong	Strong	OK	Weak
Written Daily:	Very Strong	Strong	OK	Weak

Writing

Topic Development:	Very Strong	Strong	OK	Weak
Paragraphing:	Very Strong	Strong	OK	Weak
Sentences:	Very Strong	Strong	OK	Weak
Wording:	Very Strong	Strong	OK	Weak
Revision:	Very Strong	Strong	OK	Weak
Mechanics:	Very Strong	Strong	OK	Weak
Appearance:	Very Strong	Strong	OK	Weak
Portfolio Appearance:	Very Strong	Strong	OK	Weak

In-class

Use of time:	Very Strong	Strong	OK	Weak
Listener, Questioner, & Speaker:	Very Strong	Strong	OK	Weak
Volunteer:	Very Strong	Strong	OK	Weak

OVERALL ASSESSMENT

Very Strong	Strong	OK	Weak

Numerical Assessment

———

Figure 9–1. (Continued)

I try to have all of the class members attend discussion days, but sometimes their schedules don't allow it. And yes, I offer minilessons, too. Usually these lessons focus on problems that have surfaced in the students' portfolios over the previous quarter. Here's a list I have sitting on my desk right now that we will discuss during ISP discussion days:

- meaningful and engaging titles
- review commas
- review semicolons
- journal topics
- review run-on sentences
- than and then
- eliminating words such as *very, almost, it, thing*
- when to write out numbers
- affect and effect
- underlining, italics, and bold

Minilessons and class discussions break up the fourth quarter. More important, however, these gatherings reunite us as a classroom community.

Does the Room 109 curriculum connect to Maine's Learner Standards and to the district's curriculum?
Yes. I've devised a series of sheets that match up with Maine's Learner Standards and Learner Outcomes as well as the grade-level benchmarks (see Figure 9–2). These standards inform our local curriculum. As the students fill out these forms, they are thinking about the work they have accomplished in reading, writing, speaking, listening, observing, and other language arts and life skills. The forms are, to me, proof that we are meeting and exceeding the state and local ideals.

Each student receives a complete set of these forms for their People Plans (Kent 1997, 143)—personal files that hold material relative to each student, including all the portfolio response letters. These simple checklists help me see where I might strengthen Room 109's curriculum relative to the district's; they also help my students see what they have accomplished throughout the year. Even though these forms are institutionally static, they create an awareness for both student and teacher. Let me give you an example.

This year during Stage 109, I reviewed the state standards and noticed under Speaking: "Make a formal introduction of a person." In the past students stood to introduce themselves. I moved this exercise to the next level by adding the introduction of a classmate. Students pair up and interview each other. The result is a one-minute introduction.

Such changes are basic but seem fundamental when considering the value of curriculum and *what students need to know and be able to do.*

Room 109
Identifying Standards &
Learner Outcomes

Name *Melissa Thibodeau*   Date *May 14*   Grade *11th*

Reading

Standard 1.1 Read for specific purposes (information or enjoyment).

(Good)   OK   Needs Work

Example: *I read* A Search for JD Salinger *because I am doing an independent research project on him.*

Standard 1.2 Use effective strategies to improve reading.

(Good)   OK   Needs Work

Example: *I challenged myself by reading a college-level book:* Balm in Gilead *by Sarah Lawrence Lightfoot.*

Standard 1.3 Construct meaning from text.

(Good)   OK   Needs Work

Example: *When I read* Way of the Peaceful Warrior *by Dan Millman I demonstrated a good understanding of the book by my project.*

Standard 1.4 Expand and refine understanding by integrating reading, writing, speaking, and listening.

(Good)   OK   Needs Work

Example: *I read* Letters to My Son *and made a photographic display on fathers (my father!).*

Standard 1.5 Possess a lifelong desire to read.

(Good)   OK   Needs Work

Example: *I love reading and will continue. I already read 7 books this quarter.*

Figure 9–2. Melissa's Standards and Learner Outcomes Form

Writing

Standard 2.1 Write for a variety of purposes and audiences.

(Good)   OK   Needs Work

Example: *I wrote to little kids. My parents always read my portfolios. I wrote up an interview I conducted on an elderly person and they read it.*

Standard 2.2 Communicate clearly and effectively using standard oral and written language conventions.

Good   (OK)   Needs Work

Example: *I write well, but speaking is still a bit of a problem because I am nervous. During Stage 109 I did pretty well on my demonstration.*

Standard 2.3 Use effective strategies to create and to improve writing.

(Good)   OK   Needs Work

Example: *I had my children's essay "Breaking the Mold" edited 12 times by my editor.*

Standard 2.4 Understand and utilize the writing process.

(Good)   OK   Needs Work

Example: *I usually write a few outlines before a paper and use many editing peers.*

Speaking

Standard 3.1 Adapt speaking to different audiences and purposes according to needs and expectations.

(Good)   OK   Needs Work

Example: *I spoke in front of my peers and in front of an elementary school classroom! I am getting more comfortable.*

Standard 3.2 Speak effectively in relation to five communication functions (expressing feeling, socializing, imagining, informing, and controlling).

(Good)   OK   Needs Work

Example: *When I recited "Oranges" for a poetry selection I spoke easily and smoothly.*

Figure 9–2. (Continued)

Listening

Standard 4.1 Use the stages of the listening process to understand aural messages.

(Good)   OK   Needs Work

Example: *I listen to my peers as they recite poems and passages to learn and sometimes to feel more.*

Standard 4.2 Listen for a variety of purposes.

(Good)   OK   Needs Work

Example: *At the NHS convention, I listened to be polite! In biology, I listen to learn. In Stage 109, I listen to be entertained!*

Standard 4.3 Develop a positive attitude toward listening.

(Good)   OK   Needs Work

Example: *If you have a good attitude toward listening to people, those people are more comfortable with you—they trust you.*

Language

Standard 5.1 Understand that English is one of a family of languages and is continually changing.

(Good)   OK   Needs Work

Example: *I read* Latino American—Beneath the Mangoes. *That helped me understand their culture.*

Standard 5.2 Increase knowledge of word information and enlarge vocabulary.

Good   (OK)   Needs Work

Example: *I read a lot, but I still need to use larger vocabulary in my own work (such as idiosyncratic!)*

Standard 5.3 Understand and use the structure of language, including grammatical concepts and skills.

(Good)   OK   Needs Work

Example: *Just recently I learned how to pick out all of the passive voice in my papers!*

Figure 9–2. (Continued)

Literature

Standard 6.1 Understand that literature reflects, examines, and influences the human experience.

〈 Good 〉　　　　OK　　　　Needs Work

Example: Writing Down the Bones *is a how-to on writing that relates life to words. Definitely a human experience for me.*

Standard 6.2 Develop a critical appreciation of literature.

〈 Good 〉　　　　OK　　　　Needs Work

Example: *I wrote a reaction to* The Catcher in the Rye *in which I celebrated the book as a wonderful piece of work.*

Standard 6.3 Understand how literary form and content interact to communicate meaning.

Good　　　　〈 OK 〉　　　　Needs Work

Example: *I read* Into Thin Air *which helped me learn a bit about mountain climbing.*

Standard 6.4 Develops a lifelong habit of reading.

〈 Good 〉　　　　OK　　　　Needs Work

Example: *I know I will continue to read throughout my life. I have always read a lot.*

Figure 9–2. (Continued)

Room 109
Grade 11
Benchmarks

Reading

Standard 1.3 Construct meaning from text.

(Good)   OK   Needs Work

Example: *When I read* Way of the Peaceful Warrior *I demonstrated understanding of the book by a project.*

*Recognize author's bias and prejudices.

(Good)   OK   Needs Work

Example: *I don't have an example right this minute, but I know when someone from the conservative right writes about issues that they have a certain agenda.*

Speaking

Standard 3.2 Speaks effectively in relation to five communication functions (expressing feeling, socializing, imagining, informing, and controlling)

(Good)   OK   Needs Work

Example: *When I talk about issues in class, I feel that I am honest and sincere.*

*Make a formal introduction of a person.

(Good)   OK   Needs Work

Example: *I introduced myself to class in Stage 109.*

*Participate in a panel discussion.

(Good)   OK   Needs Work

Example: *In Room 109 this is what we have every day.*

Listening

Standard 4.3 Develop a positive attitude toward listening

(Good)   OK   Needs Work

Example: *I have a good attitude toward speakers—that helps them respond to me better.*

Figure 9–2. (Continued)

*Identify some of the elements which may contribute to a shift in the overall mood in an oral presentation (chanrgesin time, location, rhythm of sentences, etc.)

<u>Good</u>   OK   Needs Work

Example: *In my play,* Cinderella Re-make, *I had to play a couple of different characters. This helped me think about different roles and all.*

*Listen in order to analyze and evaluate a presentation.

<u>Good</u>   OK   Needs Work

Example: *I listened to one presentation in class on making chocolate milk. I evaluated the person with a laugh and a nod!*

Language

Standard 5.3 Understand and use the structure of language, including grammatical concepts and skills.

<u>Good</u>   OK   Needs Work

Example: *Recently, I have learned how to eliminate passive voice from my writing.*

*Student uses commas	(YES) NO
*Student uses quotation marks	(YES) NO
*Student uses underline (italics)	(YES) NO

but sometimes I have a hard time with this not sure whether to use bold or italics.

Figure 9–2. (Continued)

What kinds of teacher research do you do to assess the effectiveness of ISP?
I listen to my students' stories. At the end of the school year, the students reflect on their time in *and* out of Room 109 (Kent 1997, 155). In one part of their final reflection, I ask them to look at their ISP experience. The following is that section along with the questions I pose to stimulate their responses:

Looking closely at Independent Study Projects

I am very interested in your thoughts about independent study. Your answers will help me fine-tune what I do and how I do it here in Room 109. Please, as always, be straightforward. Use the following questions as a guide:

- How would you approach your independent study project differently if you had this opportunity again?
- What have you learned from your study? How have you grown by having been allowed to plan, work, and create your own project?
- What did you do very well during this project? What did you do not-so well? If you were bored, why couldn't you get "un-bored"?
- Was there anything that Mr. Kent could have done better to assist with your study?

Please feel free to explore the independent study concept any way you would like. Your ideas will help me get better at offering ISP to students in the future!

Originally, I had planned to write a series of representative quotations on ISP from my students' final reflections. But then I read again this one by Katie, a junior, and decided to let her words sum up ISP for most students of Room 109.

Independent Study Project: this was a definite success. I felt so positive about what I have learned over these last nine weeks. I am proud to say that this was very beneficial. I wish I had the chance to do this kind of thing more often. Independent gave me the opportunity to seek out what I wanted. I was able to do anything, and it felt good. I felt like I was an adult for once . . .

This quarter helped me determine my future. It made me think about what I actually want from life, and what it wants from me. I am very energized about learning. I can't wait for another year. Ideas about next year's independent study have already floated in my mind. Thank you for offering such a wonderful quarter. This was a stepping stone for my future as a teacher.

Conversations with former students greatly inform my practice. Recently, I wrote an E-mail to a number quizzing them on their ISP experience. Of the replies I received three in particular, from Jason, Josie, and David, help me see the larger picture.

Earlier on in the book I wrote about Jason's multitheme ISP. Two years out of high school and in a technical college, Jason is applying to four-year schools. He answered me immediately, writing:

> *It's funny. I was reading over my ISP on art and architecture this weekend before you wrote! Anyway, did my ISP open any doors? I guess the heck so . . . I went from knowing nothing about art and just a little about architecture. My ISP opened two doors, both of which led me down a road that said "Your life will be creating." And since those two ISP, I have never had a doubt that I will create in some way for the rest of my life.*

Josie studied feminism and modern dance during her ISP. As I wrote earlier, she is now attending a performing arts college. She writes from the Netherlands, where she is spending a semester abroad:

> *. . . studying and learning about feminism and modern dance during my senior year was the start of something that has continued to shape me. Other dancers at Emerson are not as concerned about the relationship of dance to gender roles. I really do believe that a large part of my passion for the subject comes from that initial encouragement and the freedom to explore the topics I chose.*
>
> *I am very involved with the relationship of text to movement . . . I can STILL remember telling you that I couldn't choreograph to a poem, and you told me to do it anyway. And here I am!!!*

David, a three-year veteran of 109 ISP, studies secondary English teaching at Boston University. From teaching elementary students about computers at a nearby school to creating a multimedia CD on Room 109 and then again on his small town, David immersed himself in study. This future teaching star writes:

> *I have been thinking today how ISP helped me beyond the usual things like time management and communication skills . . . the freedom and personal control helped my confidence. The ISP takes the focus off the teacher and places it on the student. When I was able to create multimedia for class, I was excited and driven. I had a goal and a reason to do all the work. In the end, I was able to teach elementary kids multimedia. I felt important, and I wanted to learn more to teach more. There was a reason to learn. This helped me make my decision to pursue education at BU.*

Over the years do you have a favorite ISP?
Teachers don't have favorites. (Tim and his dad's twenty-foot sailboat. It was so cool to watch father and son working together. This boat is the best. So are they.)

10

Beyond Tomorrow

"Here's a great book," I say, holding a copy of Judy Blume's *Forever*, a sure-fire winner for girls who are reluctant readers.

Even after I had explained the story and let her read the dust cover, Andi looked at me as if I had suggested she shave her head. "Nope. Sounds boring."

That was September.

Pretty much the same happened throughout the rest of the fall and winter. Andi read a few short stories and with her good friend, Susan, she seemed to have read all or the better part of *The Acorn People* by Ron Jones. Small break-throughs to be sure, but not the one to push Andi to the status of reader.

In February while checking on some of my students in the media center, I discovered Andi and Susan holed up in the far corner devouring a large book about dog breeds. I'd never seen them so intent and focused. I suggested they do their independent study project on animals. I added that they could visit the local veterinarian—my brother, Fred—and also spend time at the animal shelter.

Andi became a reader during her independent study project. When she wasn't out of school caring for animals, she had her nose in a book about them. From a score of brochures and Internet writings to *All Creatures Great and Small* by James Herriot, Andi immersed herself in reading. She even began book-talking with me: "Did you know that President Kennedy used to talk with his Welsh Terrier, Charlie?"

In June, Andi's mom rushed to my side at graduation. "Do you know what she wanted for graduation? Do you know?"

I knew, for Andi had already finished reading her graduation book and written a blurb for our Books of 109 site. She posted her message two days *after* the seniors were through with school.

Why We Love the Dogs We Do by Stanley Coren is one of the best books I have ever read. If you're thinking about getting a dog, you need to read this. If you're thinking about working with dogs, you need to read this book, too.

Endless Possibilities

I know that Josie would still be attending a performing arts college even if she hadn't studied modern dance during the last quarter of English. I also know that Ryan and Chad would be enrolled in pre-med regardless of ISP; that Allana would be a poet, Jason a game warden, and Jess a secretary.

At the same time, I know working in an elementary school during ISP changed Ben's career path. In fact, just the other day Ben received word he had been accepted into the Saint Joseph's College elementary education program. In just a few years Ben may be managing his own class of elementary school kids. Would he, and others, be as focused and excited about their futures had ISP not come their way? Perhaps, but I know the program makes a difference.

College Essays: Aaron's Story

Scores of college essays have been written about ISP by my students. Aaron's independent study project on diversity gave him much to reflect upon. The following is an excerpt from one of his college essays:

> Growing up in a rural mill town tucked away in the foothills of western Maine seems almost storybook. Rumford provides its people with the safe, peaceful atmosphere that most only dream of. Granted, it's nothing extravagant. We don't have a mall, a movie theater, or even a Wal-Mart. For many people, Rumford is an ideal place to settle down, live, and perhaps raise a family. My hometown has many admirable qualities, but diversity is among the missing.
>
> Last year, as a junior, I decided to use my last quarter in English exploring issues of diversity with a focus on homosexuality. Once I began reading and talking about diversity with a number of people, the possibilities seemed endless. Researching a controversial issue such as this was a difficult task within my rural community; traveling to more urban regions of the state proved important.
>
> I devoted those eight weeks to my independent study project. Books such as *When Someone You Know is Gay* by Susan and Daniel Cohen, *Honor Bound* by Joseph Steffan, and *The Shared Heart* by Adam Mastoon led me to think about sexual difference. Surveying students at my school opened my eyes to the way Rumford's youth viewed those with a sexual orientation other than heterosexual. Furthermore, conducting interviews with both a Catholic priest and a lesbian college professor gave me some of the varied viewpoints on homosexuality. Ultimately, this project provided me with the type of hands-on learning that could never be achieved in a classroom alone.

The lack of diversity I experienced growing up remains an obstacle sheltering me from life outside our valley. My independent study project broadened my horizons and allowed many experiences; however, this is only the beginning. College is the next step in my growth as an accepting and diverse person. Living among a variety of people in college on a daily basis will be my final preparation for life in the world beyond my hometown.

College Interviews

Aaron's experiences with his independent study project gave him much to discuss when he interviewed at the University of Virginia, William and Mary, and American University. Surely, many of my students use their independent study projects as focal points for their college interviews. These experiences set them apart from the crowd, especially when they bring along an ISP portfolio, a photo album, or a project.

Jobs

Of course, ISP does not guarantee jobs. But as I write this, Jason is working for the architectural firm he visited during his ISP. Katherine is a writing center editor at her college. Chad and Ryan are emergency medical technicians; Sarah received a recommendation from the doctor she job-shadowed; Matt is directing an aquatics program. Independent study projects offer experiences and can connect young adults to the work world.

Teacher Evaluations

Because these independent study projects help me see and experience my students in a number of different arenas, I feel more qualified to write on their behalf for college and job opportunities. The following is an evaluation I wrote for Katie at the beginning of her senior year:

Teacher Evaluation
of Katie Doucette

At Meroby Elementary School, Katie moves among her young protégés with grace and the ease of a professional. When she speaks to her high school classmates about this independent study teaching experience, she has the confidence of a college intern.

On the soccer pitch, she streaks down the right touchline, bending her run, eyeing yet one more shot on goal during an all-star season. As captain of the conference champions, she is a role model for all levels of players. And more, little girls in our valley want to grow up to *be* Katie Doucette.

I have known Katie and her family for many years. Her older sister, Andrea

(Colby College '98), is a former student; her hardworking folks, Jane and Kim, are highly-respected members of our community. For the past two years, I have been Katie's English teacher and her advisor in The Writing Center. As the boys' varsity soccer coach, I have worked with Katie on the pitch and have witnessed her powerful play in numerous matches. In every circumstance Katie carries herself with poise and energy.

As a writer, Katie has an inviting voice. She enjoys looking closely at subjects while revealing all sides. Katie has a balanced approach to writing as she does to life. She sees all sides of issues and knows how to capture them in words. Recently, Katie wrote a brilliant reflection of her time teaching in an elementary school. Touching and intelligent, this winning essay will remain with me for a long time to come. In my letter response to her independent study project and this particular essay, I wrote:

"'My Learning Experiences' is a thoughtful reflection that has an energy for life and learning . . . This entire essay shows a full range of understanding. It is a learning testimonial; a learner's life story. With this essay you have taken a giant step as a writer and thinker."

A skilled editor, Katie guides her charges through the revision process. She maintains a fine relationship with her own editor and always seeks to refine her written work. As a writer in college, Katie will be judicious—often, she will make her professors smile. Katie has heart; at times, she reveals wisdom.

As a reader, Katie challenges herself with a variety of rich books. From Frankl's *Man's Search for Meaning* to Dillard's *A Writer's Life*, this young woman selects books that open her mind and challenge her understanding. Katie's grasp of these books is impressive; often her commentaries on these readings reveal her emerging scholarship. When presenting on her readings, Katie is organized and entertaining.

As a speaker, Katie is poised in front of large and small groups. She has a way of transferring her energy to her audience. She holds our attention and makes us care. In fact, in response to her independent study project presentation last June, I wrote:

"When you presented in front of the class on learning/teaching/ education, you had the sophistication, poise, and insight of an adult college student. I was impressed by the way you spoke, and proud of the knowledge and confidence you displayed. Your presentation will remain a highlight of my year. Thank you."

Katie's artistic projects in celebration of her readings are experimental and show adventurousness—and each is stunning. After reading the book *Titanic*, Katie set out to paint her first oil on canvas. Framed in black wood, this brooding picture captures the final moments of the fateful voyage. I hope this picture will always hang in my classroom; if not, it will forever occupy a place in my memory as a testament to the work of a dazzling human being.

At this writing, Katie is looking seriously at a career in teaching. Her work thus far in the younger grades convinces me that she is a natural. In fact, in my final letter to her last year I wrote, "If you were to enter the teaching profession, we would be graced. You are a gift, Katie." I believed that then; I am absolutely convinced of it now.

Finally, if I were given the pleasure of selecting people for a college community, here is why I would select Katie. She works hard and gives her best. She has a common sense intelligence and always looks to find meaning. Because of her rich, wonderful personality, she brings out *our* best. The bottom line? She is a complete person who is interested and interesting; a person I would want my daughter or son to enjoy as a friend, a classmate, or a teacher. Indeed, any college will be graced with Katie Doucette among its students.

I offer this evaluation with unwavering enthusiasm and with all of my heart.

Richard Kent, Teacher of English

It is not uncommon for me to add the words of ISP mentors into a student's evaluation. I will call or write the person and ask for a few words. The following is an example by my friend, Kathy Kellogg, a third-grade teacher:

In the time Sam An has spent in my third-grade classroom, he has enriched my students' lives through his creativity, sensitivity, perceptiveness, and teaching savvy. This beautiful human being has the keen skills of teaching that take many educators years to acquire."

And so …

Each teaching day I think of ways to connect the world beyond the classroom door to my students.

This morning, as usual on snowy days, small groups of senior citizens hiked our hallways for exercise. As they paraded by, I thought how valuable it would be to have three or four of them interview my students about their projects. Imagine being sixteen years old and having three or four grandparent types raving about your school work.

At lunch, I read a notice in our local newspaper. The Service Corps of Retired Executives is offering its free services to local businesspeople. Perhaps they could help some of my students find internships?

This afternoon, when J. D. came into my classroom, it dawned on me that this twenty-something-year-Navy-veteran-turned-first-floor-custodian would be a great resource for the independent study project Josh is proposing.

And this evening, just a few weeks away from the beginning of ISP, I was cruising an Internet bookseller and came across an extraordinary list of books on baseball. I immediately E-mailed one of my baseball playing students.

Matthew replied, "That's seriously what I wanted to do for independent, but I didn't really know if baseball was too broad or unoriginal."

And so, in a few weeks Matthew and the others will be on their way. Some will attack, others will stroll, and a few will sit down to rest before the journey begins.

What better lesson, for this is the way of life beyond our classroom.

Appendix
At-a-Glance ISP Outlines

Research/Academic Studies ISP
Title: Books and Their Movies

Description: Comparing and contrasting books and their movies

Suggested Reading:
Gone with the Wind (Margaret Mitchell)
Of Mice and Men (John Steinbeck)
This Boy's Life (Tobias Wolff)
On Screen Writing (Edward Dmytryk)
Television and Screen Writing: From Concept to Contract (Richard A. Blum)

Suggested Writings:
A character analysis of the book character and then the movie character
What did the screen writer choose to keep in the movie and why
A magazine article à la Siskel and Ebert rating the book and the movie
An outline of the book's major scenes side-by-side with an outline of the movie's scenes

Audio-visual Resources: Each book's movie

Web Site: www.amazon.com

Out-of-school Activities:
Visit the local video store
Visit the local bookstore and library
Interview a film critic
Interview a college professor of film and theater or an English professor

In-school Activities:
Search for articles on movie-book comparisons
Interview students or staff members concerning movie-book comparisons
Make a flannel board with movie-book comparisons
Paint a mural of famous book-movie pairs

Presentation:
Read a portion from a novel and then show the same short scene in the movie
Show the outline of a book as compared to the honed down outline of the movie
Dramatize one part of a book-movie
Talk about a book that has not been made into a movie and how it might be
Enter into a discussion with classmates about their experience with book-movie pairs

Title: Creating a Web Page

Description: A study and creation of Web pages for the Internet

Suggested Reading:
The Complete Idiot's Guide to Creating an Html 4 Web Page (Paul McFedries)
10 Minute Guide to Html 4.0 (Tim Evans)
Html 4.0: No Experience Required (E. Stephen MacK, Janan Platt, Stephen Mack)

Suggested Writings:
Day-to-day journaling of experience—the pitfalls and the solutions
Compose the script for the multimedia presentation
An essay on computers and the world today and tomorrow
Where will the Internet take us in the future
Older folks and computers

Audio-visual Resources:
Learn How to Build a Web Page (Vol. 1 and 2); VIDEO
Build Your Own Web Page; VIDEO

Web Sites:
www.builder.com
www.w3.org/markup/guide/
www.voyager.co.nz/~bsimpson/html.htm

Out-of-school Activities:
Job-shadow a Web page designer
Intern at a computer store
Job-shadow a corporate computer specialist

In-school Activities:
Create your own Web page
Work at the computer lab
Job-shadow the school district's computer coordinator
Search the Internet

Presentation:
Show Web page produced
Explain the process
Talk about the job prospects

Title: The Beatles

Description: A look at the life and times of the Beatles

Suggested Reading:
Paul McCartney: Many Years from Now (Barry Mills)
Imagine—John Lennon (Andrew Solt and Sam Egan)
She Loves You (Elaine Segal)
The Beatles: A Diary (Barry Miles)
The Complete Idiot's Guide to the Beatles (Richard Buskin)

Suggested Writings:
Paper on the conversion of a tour band to studio band
A biography of each Beatle
An analysis of a Beatle song
The Beatles: The Effect on Rock-'n'-Roll
Interview of a Beatles' fan of the 1960s

Audio-visual Resources:
The Beatles music collections
Beatles movies

Web Site: www.best.com/~abbeyrd

Out-of-school Activities:
Visit music stores
Interview members of a rock group concerning the Beatles' influence on music
Interview older people who feel the Beatles hurt society
Interview a college music professor

In-school Activities:
Interview a music teacher
Interview a history teacher
Create a mobile of the Beatles

Presentation:
Play music
Discuss influence
Have a sing-a-long of Beatles favorites
Hang a mobile and describe its features
Show a video clip of the Beatles on the Ed Sullivan Show

Title: Gay/Lesbian/Bisexual/Transgender

Description: A study of gay/lesbian/bisexual/transgender issues

Suggested Reading:
When Someone You Know is Gay (Susan and Daniel Cohen)
The Shared Heart (Adam Mastoon)
Honor Bound (Joseph Steffan)
Growing Up Gay/Growing Up Lesbian (Bennett L. Singer, editor)
You Know You're Gay When . . . (Joseph Cohen)

Suggested Writings:
Synthesis of a survey on gay/lesbian issues
Recount the interview with a gay or lesbian
"What if the majority of the world were homosexual and you were heterosexual?"
Write reactions to the gay teenagers' stories in *The Shared Heart*
Write the short story of a young person "coming out" to her or his friends
Write a dictionary of gay terms
Write an editorial for school newspaper about tolerance

Audio-visual Resources:
Torch Song Trilogy; VIDEO
To Wong Foo, Thanks for Everything! Julie Newmar; VIDEO
The Birdcage; VIDEO

Web Sites:
www.galebc.org/
www.ngltf.org/
www.rmc.library.cornell.edu

Out-of-school Activities:
Interview a gay/lesbian person
Sit in on a human sexuality class at a college
Interview a psychologist

In-school Activities:
Survey students on tolerance
Interview staff about their experiences with gay students
Read school and state policies about sexual harassment

Presentation:
Offer statistics concerning percentage of gay people
Talk about suicide among gay teens
Give resources to consult about gay issues
Role play a "coming out" scene

Title: Men and Women Relationships

Description: A study of the differences and similarities of men and women

Suggested Reading:
Men Are from Mars, Women Are from Venus (John Gray)
You Just Don't Understand: Conversation Between Men and Women (Deborah Tannen)
Couplehood (Paul Reiser)
Tales My Father Never Told (Walter Dumaux Edmonds)
Men and Women (Peter Swerdloff)

Suggested Writings:
Put together a booklet of successful dating tips for teenagers
Interview a couple married for 40-plus years; what makes their relationship work
Write a synthesis of comments by teenagers about relationships
Write a poem about the opposite sex

Audio-visual Resources:
Shadowlands; the movie biography of C. S. Lewis
On Golden Pond; VIDEO
Romeo and Juliet; VIDEO

Web Sites:
www.relationshipexpert.com
www.marsvenus.com

Out-of-school Activities:
Observing behavior of the sexes in malls, restaurants, and schools
Interviewing couples
Going to a college Women's Center

In-school Activities:
Interview students in cafeteria about relationships
Interview staff members
Internet searches
Search media center for books and audio/video material

Presentation:
Video of couples talking
Ask questions that would stimulate thinking and discussion
Collage of movie moments

Title: Opera

Description: The study of opera through reading and listening

Suggested Reading:
Opera for Dummies (David Pogue, Scott Speck)
100 Great Opera and Their Stories (Henry W. Simon)
The Phantom of the Opera (Gaston Leroux, original novel)

Suggested Writings:
Tell the story of an opera in a modern-day short story
Relate an interview with a professional musician
Write about or analyze a piece of music
Write a song or poem in celebration of an opera
Keep a journal of the ISP experience

Audio-visual Resources:
Andrew Lloyd Webber—The Premiere Collection Encore (1992); VIDEO
Phantom of the Opera (1925)—Chaney; VIDEO
Barber of Seville—Comp Opera; VIDEO
The Best of Italian Opera; Giusseppe Verdi (Composer); CD
Cats/Phantom of the Opera; Andrew Lloyd Webber; CD

Web Sites:
www.amazon.com
www.gray.music.rhodes.edu/Musichtmls/bfproj.html
http://dir.yahoo.com/Arts/Performing_Arts/Opera/Opera_Companies/

Out-of-school Activities:
Go to a college music recital
Attend a concert
Interview musicians
Visit a music store
Visit the music section of a large bookstore
Visit a classic radio station
Interview the conductor of a symphony

In-school Activities:
Internet research
Interview music director
Interview band members
Develop a survey for staff and community members about opera
Read scripts of operas from the Internet

Presentation:
Video collage of various operas
Audio collage of different operas
Invite a musician to play and discuss music
Photos of various experiences
Teach different kinds of operas

Career ISP

Title: Athletic Trainer

Description: A study of the education and the life of an athletic trainer

Suggested Reading:
Principles of Athletic Training (Arnheim/Prentice)
Essentials in Athletic Training (Arnheim/Prentice)
Fitness for Dummies (IDG Books)

Suggested Writings:
Life as a . . .
> College athletic trainer
> High school trainer
> Pro team athletic trainer
> Gym trainer
> Private/personal trainer
> Work in a hospital, physical therapist office

Education needed
Interview of an athletic trainer
Interview coaches and athletes
New trends in injury prevention and injury recovery

Web Sites:
www.nata.org (National Athletic Trainers' Association)
www.csulb.edu/~athtrain
www.mnu.edu/behav_sci/ath_training/

Out-of-school Activities:
Job-shadow an athletic trainer
Interview college coaches
Interview athletes, both amateur and professional

In-school Activities:
Interview athletes who have worked with trainers during recovery periods
Interview coaches and physical education teachers

Presentation:
Bring in an athletic trainer's kit
Talk about prevention and care
Demonstrate taping techniques
Talk about injury recovery using stretching and other techniques

Title: Business

Description: A study of life in the business world

Suggested Reading:
The Millionaire Next Door (Thomas J. Stanley, William D. Danko)
Winnie-the-Pooh on Success (Roger E. Allen, Stephen D. Allen)
Business Week magazine
Wall Street Journal newspaper
USA Today newspaper business section
Read the biography of any successful businessperson (e.g., Bill Gates, Howard Hughes)

Suggested Writings:
Letters to businesspeople to inquire about obtaining a one-day internship
Credo of business ethics
Essays on specific jobs
Essays on various visitations
Write a biography of a successful businessperson

Audio-visual Resources:
Great Minds of Business; (Fred Smith et al.); VIDEO
Building a Successful Business; (Video Presentations); VIDEO

Web Site: www.all-biz.com

Out-of-school Activities:
Job-shadow, intern, or apprentice
Interview people in a business, from the lower echelon to president/manager
Visit a school of business at a college/university
Visit a college placement bureau
Visit the Better Business Bureau
Visit the local chamber of commerce
Talk with people at the local Rotary Club

In-school Activities:
Visit school district business manager
Interview business education teacher
Interview students and staff who have started their own businesses
Develop a crossword puzzle using business terms

Presentation:
Develop your own advertisement campaign for a business
Produce a commercial
Discuss the top jobs in the U.S. today

Title: Mind/Body Spiritual Healing

Description: A study of alternative medicine and the relationship between the mind and the body

Suggested Reading:
Hands of Light: A Guide to Healing Through the Human Energy Field (Barbara Ann Brennan, Joseph A. Smith, illustrator)
Healing Emotions: Conversations with the Dalai Lama on Mindfulness, Emotions, and Health (Daniel Goleman, editor)
Your Sacred Self (Wayne W. Dyer)
Alternative Medicine for Dummies (James Dillard, Terra Diane Ziporyn)
Radical Healing (Rudolph Ballentine)

Suggested Writings:
An essay on the alternative medicine practices
An essay on acupuncture
Poem about mind/body connection
Keep a journal of various experiences

Audio-visual Resources:
Anatomy of Spirit: The Seven Stages of Power and Healing (Caroline Myss)

Web Site: dir.yahoo.com/Health/Alternative_Medicine/

Out-of-school Activities:
Take a course at a hospital or college
Visit a massage therapist
Talk with an Auyurvedic doctor
Meet with a priest

In-school Activities:
Reading
Internet research
Discuss mind/body connection with biology and psychology teachers
Write a manual depicting various spiritual practices

Presentation:
Talk about the mind/body connection
Show a drawing of the various energy paths in the body
Present a scrapbook of various experiences
Teach basic shoulder massage and have class perform on one another

Title: Administrative Assistant

Description: Study the career life of an administrative assistant

Suggested Reading:
The Administrative Assistant (Brenda Bailey-Hughes)
Empower Yourself! A Take-Charge Assistant Book (Marlene Caroselle)
Administrative Assistant's & Secretary's Handbook (James Stroman, et al.)
Will the Real Boss Please Stand Up? Taking Your Administrative Career to the Next Level (George-
   Anne Fay)

Suggested Writings:
Short story of an incredible day as the school principal's administrative assistant
Essay depicting the various responsibilities of an administrative assistant
Informational essay on education necessary
What is an administrative assistant
What's an executive secretary

Audio-visual Resources:
9 to 5
Secret of My Success
Working Girl

Web Site: www.alliedschools.com/html/secretary_2_faq.html

Out-of-school Activities:
Job-shadow a variety of administrative assistants (e.g., law, medical, corporate)
Visit a business school
Discuss job prospects with placement agency
Talk with an executive about the qualities of an effective (indispensable) administrative
   assistant

In-school Activities:
Work in the school's office
Interview the school's business teacher
Interview the school district's secretarial staff
Try transcribing from a Dictaphone system
Talk with the guidance counselor or career counselor

Presentation:
Review the responsibilities of an administrative assistant
Develop a bulletin board depicting the various fields for administrative assistants
Present a skit with a boss and her/his administrative assistant that helps depict the import
   of the position

Title: The Writer's Life

Description: The study of being an author, from writing magazine articles to novels. This ISP includes working to improve the student's own writing.

Suggested Reading:
Writing Down the Bones (Natalie Goldberg)
Description (Monica Wood)
The Writing Life (Annie Dillard)
If You Want to Write (Brenda Ueland)
Wild Mind (Natalie Goldberg)
Author biographies
  F. Scott Fitzgerald (Howard Greenfield)
  John Steinbeck (Richard O'Connor)
  Harriet Beecher Stowe (Suzanne M. Coil)
Writing magazines (*The Writer; Writer's Digest*)

Suggested Writings:
Work with an author or editor over time revising a piece of writing
Create a synthesis of the helpful hints from various books on writing
Write a poem about finding the right word
Write a short story using different points of view: first person, second person, third-person omniscient, third-person limited
Write a short story from the opposite sex's point of view, from an animal's point of view, from someone who is much older
Write a blurb for a book
Write a five-minute play

Audio-visual Resources:
The Afterglow: A Tribute to Robert Frost; VIDEO
The Language of Life: A Bill Moyer's Special; VIDEO
Famous Authors Series; VIDEO
Shadowlands (C. S. Lewis story); VIDEO

Web Sites:
www.aci-plus.com
www.owl.english.purdue.edu

Out-of-school Activities:
Interview an author
Attend a reading
Attend a book signing
Attend a writing class at a college
Visit a college writing center

In-school Activities:
Design a book cover replete with dust cover copy
Work in the writing center
Make a journal suggestion board with loads of journal ideas

Presentation:

Pass out and/or read a piece of writing

Talk about writing as a process, especially the revision process

Make and pass out a book mark that has good tips about writing

Put on a puppet show focusing on the writing process

Title: Police

Description: Study the life of a police officer

Suggested Reading:
Breaking and Entering: Women Cops Break the Code of Silence to Tell Their Stories from the Inside
   (Connie Fletcher)
Silhouette in Scarlet (Cherokee Paul McDonald)
Boot: An LAPD Officer's Rookie Year (William C. Dunn)
The Killing Season: A Summer Inside an LAPD Homicide Division (Miles Corwin)

Suggested Writings:
Poem about "walking the beat" or "blue lights"
Essay focused on the criminal justice academy
Recount an interview with a veteran police officer
Essay on breakthroughs in police equipment

Audio-visual Resources:
Watch a variety of police television series or police movies

Web Site: www.policescanner.com/

Out-of-school Activities:
Police car ride-along
Visit state criminal justice academy
Interview local and state police
Visit college where criminal justice is taught
Attend a university class

In-school Activities:
Interview a DARE officer
Talk to social studies teacher about various laws (e.g., search and seizure)

Presentation:
Videotape the inside of a police department
Share interviews with police officers
Show police equipment
Invite a police officer into class
Explain various police procedures

Title: Teaching in the Younger Grades

Description: An opportunity to study the craft of teaching by working as a student teacher or teacher assistant kindergarten through sixth grade

Suggested Reading:
You Can't Say You Can't Play (Vivian Gussin Paley)
The Boy Who Would Be a Helicopter (Vivian Gussin Paley)
Teacher (Sylvia Ashton Warner)
The One Place (The Young & Rubicam Foundation)
A Letter to Teachers (Vito Perrone)

Suggested Writings:
Personal letters to students in response to their writing
In-class observation journal
Essay over a problem encountered while working with a student
Interview with teachers and principals

Audio-visual Resources:
Listening to Children—A Moral Journey with Robert Coles
Though the following do not deal with elementary school teachers, these movies on video do show the influence of teachers:
Dead Poets' Society
Goodbye Mr. Chips
To Sir with Love
Stand and Deliver
Mr. Holland's Opus
Dangerous Minds

Web Sites:
www.teachinglearning.com
www.stanford.edu
www.ucla.edu

Out-of-school Activities:
Work in an elementary school
Visit a private school
Interview a college education professor
Attend an education class at a college
Interview education students

In-school Activities:
Interview teachers and principal
Internet searches

Presentation:
Photographs of experience
Video of elementary class
Talk on learning

Hobby/Life Passion ISP

Title: Gone Fishing

Description: A study on the sport of fishing

Suggested Reading:
Joe and Me: An Education in Fishing and Friendship (James Prosek)
Trout Bam (Gary LaFontain)
Distant Waters (Valentine Atkinson)
Sex, Death, and Fly Fishing (John Gierach)
Outdoor Life magazine
The Complete Idiot's Guide to Fishing Basics (Mike Toth)

Suggested Writings:
Why "Catch and Release" is popular
Favorite fishing spots
How to tie flies and when to use which one
Best day of fishing
Journals of fishing trips

Audio-visual Resources:
A River Runs Through It; VIDEO
Complete Fishing with John: Hook Line; VIDEO
Basic Fly Fishing; ESPN Outdoor; VIDEO

Web Sites:
www.fishing.com
www.outdoorlife.com

Out-of-school Activities:
Fish different spots
Visit a fish hatchery
Talk with experienced fisherman
Talk with a guide
Interview a game warden
Visit a fish and tackle shop
Build a flat-bottomed canoe

In-school Activities:
Make maps of fishing areas
Read about best fishing spots from state magazines
Interview student and staff fisherpeople
Draw a fish

Presentation:
Discuss different equipment
Tie a fly
Show fly-fishing techniques

Title: Nature Writing

Description: A look into the natural world through reading, writing, and exploration

Suggested Reading:
This Incomparable Lande (Thomas J. Lyon)
The Norton Book of Nature Writing (Robert Finch and John Elder, eds.)
Words from the Land (Stephen Trimble, ed.)
Walden (Henry David Thoreau)
American Nature Writing 1999 (John A. Murray, ed.)

Suggested Writings:
Nonfiction narrative
Nature poem
Short story with nature setting
Interview a forest ranger or game warden
Journal of walks in the woods

Audio-visual Resources:
Lost on a Mountain in Maine (Donn Fendler); audio book
A River Runs Through It (Norman MacLean); audio book

Web Site: www.centenial.k12.mn.us/chs/english/index.html

Out-of-school Activities:
Interview a forest ranger or game warden
Walk the woods
Interview forester at local paper mill
Visit a game preserve
Go birding with a birder

In-school Activities:
Build a rock wall on school grounds
Weave a nature scene
Prepare a graph depicting nature troubles in state
Draw a cartoon of a nature issue

Presentation:
Display pictures
Read part of nonfiction narrative or poem
Give a lesson on kinds of birds, including their songs
Lead your class on a nature walk

Title: Zen and the Art of Mountain Biking

Description: The study of mountain biking from the Zen perspective

Suggested Reading:
Dirt (John Howard)
Zen and the Art of Motorcycle Maintenance (Robert M. Pirsig)
The Mountain Bike Experience (David King and Michael Kaminer)
Sacred Journey of the Peaceful Warrior (Dan Millman)
The Complete Book of Mountain Biking (Brant Richards and Steve Worland)
Mountain Bike Magic (Rob Van der Plas)
Mountain bike magazines

Suggested Writings:
Essay, poem, song—"The perfect ride"
Interview of a pro mountain biker
Synthesis of comments by mountain bikers about the sport
Biography of professional mountain biker
Handbook: The ten best rides in the area

Audio-visual Resources:
Great Mountain Biking Video; VIDEO
Ultimate Mountain Biking; VIDEO
Performance Mountain Biking; VIDEO

Web Site: www.mtbinfo.com

Out-of-school Activities:
Mountain bike a variety of places
Visit bike shop interview owner and worker
Attend a mountain bike race
Visit a mountain bike park
Intern at a bike shop or park

In-school Activities:
Build a mountain bike model
Design a mountain bike park out of papier maché
Paint or draw the rush of mountain biking
Interview students and staff who mountain bike

Presentation:
Give talk on history
Show video of races
Discuss bike maintenance
Hand out ten best rides handbook

Title: Learning to Draw

Description: Using a collection of drawing books, learn to draw

Suggested Reading:
Drawing on the Right Side of the Brain (Betty Edwards)
Drawing on the Artist Within (Betty Edwards)
The Zen of Seeing: Seeing Drawing as Meditation (Frederick Frank)
The Natural Way to Draw (Kimon Nicolaides)

Suggested Writings:
An essay on the right brain
Biography of an artist
Interview of an artist
Journal: life of an artist

Audio-visual Resources:
Vincent and Theo; VIDEO (the life of Vincent Van Gogh)
Watercolor Painting; Bob Fagan; VIDEO
Secrets of Painting on Location; Bob Fagan; VIDEO
Sister Wendy's Story of Painting; VIDEO (set)
PBS "How to Paint" programs

Web Site: www.miningco.com (at prompt, type "drawing and sketching")

Out-of-school Activities:
Interview an artist
Attend college drawing class
Paint or draw a scene in the woods
Go to an art museum
Attend an artist's opening at a gallery

In-school Activities:
Interview the art teacher
Interview art students
Paint or draw a mural on class wall or in corridor
Keep a sketch book

Presentation:
Guide students through a series of drawing exercises
Present drawings
Talk about the right brain

Title: Snowboarding

Description: The history, growth, and techniques of snowboarding

Suggested Reading:
The Complete Snowboarder (Jeff Bennett and Scott Downey)
Snowboarding to Nirvana (Frederick Lenz)
The Snowboarder's Total Guide to Life (Bill Kerig)
The Illustrated Guide to Snowboarding (Kevin Ryan)
(Sick) A Cultural History of Snowboarding (Susanna Howe)
The Snowboard: A Guide For All Boarders (Lowell Hart)

Suggested Writings:
Historical overview
Interview of pro snowboarder
Personal experiences as a snowboarder
Song of snowboarding freedom
Journal a boarder's day
Equipment maintenance

Audio-visual Resources:
Snowboarding 101: How to Snowboard; VIDEO
Old School—The First Competition; VIDEO
Snowboarding to Nirvana (Frederick Lenz); audio book

Web Sites:
www.snowboarding.com
www.aboutsnowboarding.com/

Out-of-school Activities:
Interview pro snowboarder
Interview teacher of sport
Visit a mountain resort
Take a lesson
Enter or attend a race

In-school Activities:
Interview snowboarders in school club (team)
Design and build a scale model snowboard park

Presentation:
Discuss growth of sport
Bring in different kinds of boards
Video collage of snowboarding
Give a lesson demonstration
Have a drawing for a free lesson at local ski area snowboard park

Title: Buddhism

Description: A look into the Buddhist tradition

Suggested Reading:
Buddha for Beginners (Stephen T. Asona)
Awakening the Buddha Within: Tibetan Wisdom for the Western World (Lama Surya Das)
That's Funny, You Don't Look Buddhist (Sylvia Boorstein)
Zen and the Art of Motorcycle Maintenance (Robert M. Pirsig)
Living Buddha, Living Christ (Thich Nhat Hann)
Mind in Buddhism (Kent Sandvik)
Buddhism (Madhu Bazaz Wangu)

Suggested Writings:
The struggles of Tibet
The Dali Lamas
The three pillars of Zen
Using Zen in everyday American life

Audio-visual Resources:
Seven Years in Tibet; VIDEO
Little Buddha; VIDEO
Requiem for a Faith: Tibetan Buddhism; VIDEO

Web Sites:
www.buddhanet.net
www.buddhism-buddha.com/

Out-of-school Activities:
Visit a Buddhist Temple
Talk with a Buddhist Family
Practice meditation
Hike to a place of solitude and journal

In-school Activities:
Paint a mural in school celebrating the Buddhist tradition
Interview any students or staff who are Buddhists

Presentation:
Discuss the basics of Buddhism
Lead class in meditation
Present a papier maché Buddha
Show drawings created during hikes

Selected Reading ISP

Title: Selected Reading in 20th-Century American History

Description: A study of 20th-Century American history through literature

Suggested Reading:
The Century (Peter Jennings, Todd Brewster)
My American Century (Studs Terkel, Roberts Coles)
Centenarians: The Story of the Twentieth Century by Americans Who Lived It (Bernard Edelman, ed.)

Suggested Writings:
A first-person short story focused on one time period or happening
A poem collage in celebration of America's 20th century
Write a commercial that attempts to get people to join the military, the Peace Corps, etc.
Write a diary of an ordinary person during a time in the 20th century

Audio-visual Resources:
History of the 20th Century (MPI Home Video Series)
The Sensational; VIDEO
The Civil War; (Ken Burns); VIDEO
Glory; VIDEO

Web Sites:
www.historychannel.com
www.elibrary.com

Out-of-school Activities:
Visit a museum
Interview a historian
Interview a college history professor
Go to antique stores or yard sales and buy items from across the decades

In-school Activities:
Interview a high school history teacher
Interview people of various ages in school about different periods in America's 20th century
Watch the History Channel on television

Presentation:
Create a wall-sized time line
Present a video collage of American 20th-century history
Make a book mark that highlights each decade of the 20th century and hand out to classmates

Title: Multicultural Literature

Description: An immersion into multicultural literature

Suggested Reading:
12 Multicultural Novels: Reading and Teaching Strategies (Monica Wood)
Jesse (Gary Soto)
The House on Mango Street (Sandra Cisneros)
Shizuko's Daughter (Kyoko Mori)
Reservation Blues (Sherman Alexie)
Maus: A Survivor's Tale, Volumes I and II (Art Spiegelman)
Ellen Foster (Kay Gibbons)

Suggested Writings:
Discuss the multicultural nature of student's hometown
Essay on immigration
Book reviews
Write an editorial concerning multicultural concerns

Audio-visual Resources:
I'll Fly Away—syndicated television program on PBS
Like Water for Chocolate; VIDEO

Web Sites:
www.Amazon.com (book sellers)
www.records.ume.maine.edu/
www.barnesandnoble.com

Out-of-school Activities:
Interview college administrator in charge of minority recruitment
Discuss the importance of multicultural literature with minorities
Attend a multicultural event at a college on in a city
Go to an art museum showing multicultural pieces
Visit a city and wander through ethnic neighborhoods

In-school Activities:
Interview students and staff of color in school about books focus on their culture
E-mail representatives of various cultural organizations to solicit names of popular books

Presentation:
Present a miniplay in celebration of a particular book
Invite a person of color to talk
Show how multiculturalism touches all of us

Title: Robert Frost

Description: A study of the American poet Robert Frost

Suggested Reading:
Robert Frost (Jeffrey Meyers)
Frost: The Poet and His Poetry (David A. Sohn and Richard H. Tyre)
The Poetry of Robert Frost: The Collected Poems, Complete and Unabridged (Edward Connery Lathem, ed.)

Suggested Writings:
Select a time frame of Frost's life and discuss his poetry and his life issues
Choose a Frost poem and write an analysis of it
Select a favorite Frost poem and write a mirror poem (see "The Passionate Shepherd to His Love" by Christopher Marlowe and "The Nymph's Reply to the Shepherd" by Sir Walter Raleigh)
Select two of Frost's poems and compare them

Audio-visual Resources:
The Afterglow: A Tribute to Robert Frost; VIDEO

Web Site: www.libarts.sfasu.edu/Frost/Index.html

Out-of-school Activities:
For East Coast people, visit Frost's cabin in Vermont!
Build a poetry garden on or near school grounds with podiums or small plaques mounted with Frost poetry
Attend a poetry reading
Visit poetry section of large bookstore

In-school Activities:
Discuss Frost with English teacher(s)
Paint a mural of a Frost poem on school wall
Make corridor passes with Frost poems on one side

Presentation:
Discuss Frost's life
Read poems from certain times of Frost's life
Lead class in an analysis of a Frost poem
Play a small section of *The Afterglow: A Tribute to Robert Frost*
Lead class through poetry garden

Title: Chaos and the Cosmos

Description: A study of randomness, chaos, and the cosmos

Suggested Reading:
Chaos (James Gleick)
The Blind Watchmaker (Richard Dawkins)
The Cosmic Code (Heinz R. Pagels)
Before It Vanishes: A Packet for Professor Pagels (Robert Pack)
Einstein's Dreams (Alan Lightman)

Suggested Writings:
A poem celebrating the cosmos
Essays in response to Robert Pack's *Before It Vanishes*
Book review of *Einstein's Dreams*
A synthesis of selected quotations from the suggested reading list above
Write about this Robert Green Ingersoll quotation: "In nature there are neither rewards
    nor punishments—there are consequences."

Audio-visual Resources:
Stephen Hawking's Universe
The Day the Universe Changed (Churchill Media)
A Brief History of Time (Stephen Hawking)

Web Sites:
www.students.uiuc.edu/~ag-ho/chaos/chaos.html
http://math.bu.edu/DYSYS/chaos-game/chaos-game.html
http://tqd.advanced.org/3120/

Out-of-school Activities:
Visit a college class
Visit a planetarium
Walk the woods and journal about order, randomness, and chaos in nature
Discuss the chaos of weather with a meteorologist

In-school Activities:
Discuss the new science of chaos with a science teacher
In the art room paint a scene of how you view chaos
In the vocational area, build a model of chaos with scrap material

Presentation:
Offer every day examples of the chaos theory
Utilizing *The Blind Watchmaker*, share insights on chaos

Title: Baseball

Description: A study of baseball, its literature, and its history

Suggested Reading:
1947: When All Hell Brooke Loose in Baseball (Red Barber)
Baseball When the Grass Was Real (Donald Honig, ed.)
Early Innings: A Documentary History of Baseball, 1825–1908 (Dean A. Sullivan, ed.)
At Fenway: Dispatches from Red Sox Nation (Dan Shaughnessy)
The Boys of Summer (Roger Kahn)
Bang the Drum Slowly (Mark Harris)
Extra Innings: Baseball Poems (Lee Bennett Hopkins)

Suggested Writings:
A poem on three balls, two strikes, two on, two out, bottom of the ninth, down by one
Essay about little league baseball or T-ball
Parents' place in little league baseball
Essay about baseball in the year 2050

Audio-visual Resources:
Baseball: A Film by Ken Burns—Nine Inning Set; VIDEO

Web Site: www.majorleaguebaseball.com

Out-of-school Activities:
Visit a major league ball park and sketch portions
Interview a college baseball coach
Interview an umpire
Job-shadow in a major or minor league team's front office
Interview an elderly person about baseball back "then"

In-school Activities:
Interview school's baseball coach
Interview school staff members who are involved in Rotisserie Baseball Leagues
Learn "Casey at the Bat"

Presentation:
Recite "Casey at the Bat"
Perform "Who's on First?" (Abbott and Costello)
Give a talk on the history of baseball which includes rules changes
Bring in historical baseball artifacts
Sing "Take Me out to the Ballpark"

Works Cited

American Association of School Libraries and the Association for Educational Communications and Technology. 1998. *Information Power: Building Partnerships for Learning.* Chicago: American Library Association.

Armstrong, Michael. 1980. *Closely Observed Children.* London: Writers and Readers, in association with Chameleon Press.

Armstrong, Thomas. 1998. *Awakening Genius in the Classroom.* Alexandria, VA: Association for Supervision and Curriculum Development.

Britton, James. 1982. In *Prospect and Retrospect: Selected Essays of James Britton,* edited by Gordon Pradl. London: Heinemann.

———. 1991. Conversations at The Bread Loaf School of English. In "Coming to Know Your Classroom: Stories and Theories." Bread Loaf Mountain Campus, Ripton, Vt.

Brooks, Jacqueline Grennon, and Brooks, Martin G. 1993. *In Search of Understanding: The Case for Constructivist Classrooms.* Alexandria, VA: Association for Supervision and Curriculum Development.

Bruner, Jerome. 1986. *Toward a Theory of Instruction.* New York: Norton.

Cazden, Courtney. 1988. "Social Interaction as Scaffold: The Power and Limits of a Metaphor." In *The Word for Teaching is Learning: Essays for James Britton,* edited by Martin Lightfoot and Nancy Martin. Portsmouth, NH: Boynton/Cook.

Deporter, Bobbi, Mark Reardon, and Sarah Singer-Nourie. 1999. *Quantum Teaching: Orchestrating Student Success.* Needham Heights, MA: Allyn & Bacon.

Freedman, James O. 1991. *Dartmouth president's address to alumni council,* May 17, Hanover, N.H.

Gardner, Howard. 1983. *Frames of Mind: The Theory of Multiple Intelligences.* New York: Basic Books.

———. 1993. *Multiple Intelligences: The Theory in Practice.* New York: Basic Books.

Gatto, John Taylor. 1992. *Dumbing Us Down: The Hidden Curriculum of Compulsory Schooling.* Gabriola Island, BC: New Society Publishers.

Glesne, Corrine, and Alan Peshkin. 1992. *Becoming Qualitative Researchers: An Introduction.* White Plains, NY: Longman.

Hillocks, Jr., George. 1995. *Teaching Writing as Reflective Practice.* New York: Teachers College Press.

Kent, Richard. 1997. *Room 109: The Promise of a Portfolio Classroom.* Portsmouth, NH: Boynton/Cook.

Paley, Vivian Gussin. 1986. "On Listening to What the Children Say." *Harvard Educational Review* 56 (2): 122–131.

Martin, Nancy. 1983. *Mostly About Writing.* Portsmouth, NH: Boynton/Cook.

Meyers, James R., and Elizabeth Warner Scott. 1989. *Getting Skilled, Getting Ahead: Your Guide for Choosing a Career and a Private Career School.* Princeton, NJ: Peterson's Guides.

U.S. Department of Defense. 1998. *Military Careers: A Guide to Military Occupations and Selected Military Career Paths.* Washington, DC: U.S. Department of Defense.

U.S. Department of Labor, Bureau of Labor Statistics. 1998. *Occupational Outlook Handbook.* Washington, DC: U.S. Department of Labor.

Vygotsky, Lev S. 1978. In *Mind in Society: The Development of Higher Psychological Processes* edited by M. Cole et al. Cambridge, MA: Harvard University Press.

Wilhelm, Jeffrey D. 1997. *"You Gotta BE the Book": Teaching Engaged and Reflective Reading with Adolescents.* New York: Teachers College Press.

Index

Absence request form, 34
Abused Women's Advocacy Program, 48
Academic/research ISP, 66-68
  outlines for, 123–128
Accountability, 61
Accreditation issues, 107
Acorn People, The, 116
Administrative assistant, resources on, 132
Age, as research topic, 32-38
All Creatures Great and Small, 116
Allen, Janet, 96
Alternative medicine, resources on, 131
American history, resources on, 143
Armed Services Vocational Aptitude Battery
    (ASVAB), 80
Armstrong, Thomas, 45
Arrowhead Library System College Bound
    Reading List, 96
Assessment
  of program, 113–115
  of students, 103–104, 105–106, 118–120
Athletic trainer, resources on, 129
Authoring, resources on, 133–134
Autobiography, student, 1–2

Baseball, resources on, 147
Beatles, resources on, 125
Blume, Judy, 116
Bodily-kinesthetic intelligence, 50
Books
  resources on, 123
  as springboard for independent study, 45–47
  student suggestions for, 19-20
Brainstorming, 30-31
Breathing In, Breathing Out, 96
Britton, James, v, 9, 25, 37
Broomhall, Chummy, 28
Buddhism, resources on, 142
Business, resources on, 130

Careers
  education and, 81–82

ISP case studies of, 69–73
  fast-track, 78
  resources for ISP based on, 129–136
  searching out, 73–80
  work values exercise, 75, 97
Cary, Suzie, 9
Chaos theory, resources on, 146
Class newspaper, 20
Cohen, Susan and Daniel, 117
College applications, ISP's benefit for, 117–118
Community service, as out-of-school project, 48
Constructivism, 24–25
Coren, Stanley, 116

D.A.R.E. Role Models, 48
Dillard, Annie, 12
Dodson, Shireen, 97
Drawing, resources on, 140
Dumbing Us Down, 104

E-mail, connections through, 13–15, 20
Elementary teaching, resources on, 136
Emerson, Ralph Waldo, 90
Essays (Emerson), 90
Evaluation
  of program, 113–115
  of students, 103–104, 105–106, 118–120
  of writing, 44–45

Federal Jobs in Law Enforcement, 80
Fendler, Don, 90
Field, Shelly, 80
Final product form, sample, 59–60
Fishing, resources on, 137
Fletcher, Ralph, 96
Fonda, Henry, 32
Forever, 116
Freedman, James, 10
Frost, Robert, 45
  resources on, 145

Gardner, Howard, 45, 49

Gatto, John Taylor, iv, 104
Gay issues, resources on, 126
Geagan, Bill, 46, 90
Getting Skilled, Getting Ahead, 75
Goswami, Dixie, 41
GRE Literature in English, 94
Great Books for Boys, 97

Hall, Donald, 7
Hall, Nancy, 4
Hawkins, Lori, 80
Hepburn, Katherine, 32
Herriot, James, 116
Hobby/life passion ISP
  case study of, 83–87
  outlines for, 137–142
  suggested hobbies, 88
Honor Bound, 117
Howe, Linda, 38
Hughes, Ted, 66
*Hurricane Island Outward Bound Book of
    Readings*, 90

Independent learning, 65
Independent study projects (ISP)
  academic/research, 66–68
  accountability and, 61
  accreditation issues, 107
  aftermath of, 116–121
  assessment of, 103–104, 105–106
  assessment of program, 113–115
  career, 69–82
  community attitudes about, 101–102
  failures of and in, 103, 104
  first week of, 51–65
  hobby/life passion, 83–87
  keepers for, 53–54, 101
  letters as part of, 84, 86–87
  model forms for, 54, 57–60
  multitheme, 89–93
  opting out of, 101
  organizing, 52–64
  outlines for, 123–147
  preparing for, 1–25
  questions and concerns about, 100–115
  practicalities of, 101, 102–103
  range of, vi
  rationale for, v
  scope of, 104, 107
  student presentations, 64

suggested products for, 63, 64
suggested reading, 94–99
suggested themes for, 55
teacher organization for, 56, 61
types of, 62
Individual attention, importance of, 32–33
Information literacy, 65
  standards of, 64–65
*Information Power: Building Partnerships for
    Learning*, 64
Interpersonal intelligence, 50
Interviews
  college, ISP's benefit for, 118
  by students, 19
Intrapersonal intelligence, 50
It's Never Too Late, 96

Jacchino, Jack, 4–5, 6
Jobs, ISP's benefit for, 118
Jones, Ron, 116

Keepers, 26, 101
  communication with, 53
Kennedy, John F., 116
Kiesman, Jerry, 101
Kingston, Maxine Hong, 12

Liability issues, 100
Life Work stories, 3–9
Linguistic-verbal intelligence, 49
Logical-mathematical intelligence, 49
Lost on a Mountain in Maine, 90

Mastoon, Adam, 117
Maus, 46
Men and women relationships, resources on,
    127
Military Careers, 80
Mosquito Test, The, 46
Mountain biking, resources on, 139
Movies, resources on, 123
Multicultural literature, resources on, 144
Multimedia packages, constructing, 22
Multiple intelligences, 45, 48–50
Multitheme ISP, case study of, 89–93
Musical-rhythmic intelligence, 50
My Neck of the Woods, 90

National Book Foundation, 96
Naturalist intelligence, 49

Nature I Loved, 46, 90
Nature writing, resources on, 138

Observation, fostering, 26–27
Occupational Outlook Handbook, 73–78
Odean, Kathleen, 97
On Golden Pond, 32
100 Best Careers for Writers and Artists, 80
100 Books for Girls to Grow On, 97
100 Jobs in Technology, 80
Opera, resources on, 128
Out-of-school projects
  keepers for, 26
  range of, 29–32
  ski area case study of, 27–29
  tutoring project case study of, 38–44

Paley, Vivian Gussin, 12
Peer Helpers, 48
Pen pals, 9–12
  benefits of, 12–13
Peters, Dorothy, 18
Plath, Sylvia, 66
Poe, Edgar Allan, 46
Police, resources on, 135
Portfolios, 8–9
  out-of-school projects in, 45–46
  responding to, 21–22
Pretty Girls in Little Boxes, 45
Prospect and Retrospect, 37
Prospectus, sample 57

Reading, resources on, 143–147
Reluctant readers, 116
Rich, Louise Dickinson, 46, 90
Rief, Linda, 96
Ryan, Joan, 45

St. John, Pete, 21
School
  guest speakers in, 22
  life skills room of, 22
  student involvement in, 15–23
Seeking Diversity: Language Arts with Adolescents, 96
Service Corps of Retired Executives
  (SCORE), 120
Shared Heart, The, 117

Sizer, Theodore, iv
Snowboarding, resources on, 141
Social responsibility, 65
Spatial-visual intelligence, 49
Spiegelman, Art, 46
Steffan, Joseph, 117
Students
  autobiographies of, 1–2
  book suggestions of, 19–20, 98–99
  involvement in school, 15–23
  making connections with, 2–3
  out-of-school projects by, 26–50
  performance by, 21
  preparing for the future, 3–9
  preparing for ISP, 23–24
  relationships with younger grades, 17–18,
    38–44
  as research assistants, 21
  volunteering by, 21
  work opportunities for, 21, 22
Suggested reading ISP, 94–97
  outlines for, 143–147
  suggested books for, 98–99

Teaching, resources on, 136
Thoreau, Henry David, 46, 89, 90, 93
Three-week check-up, sample form, 58
Turnbull, Jeff, 27
Tutoring, 17–18
  assessing, 41–44
  as out-of-school project, 38–41

Volunteers, in classroom, 18–19
Vygotsky, Lev, 25

Walden, 90
We Took to the Woods, 46, 90
Web page construction, 22
  resources on, 124
When Someone You Know Is Gay, 117
Why We Love the Dogs We Do, 116
Wilhelm, Jeffrey, 69
Women's National Book Association, 96
Wood, Anne, 18
Work values exercise, 75, 79
Writing, assessing process of, 44-45